"A GODLY MAN?
WHO CAN FIND ONE?"

—⚡—

BY

Pat Mallory

TABLE OF CONTENTS

—⁓—

INTRODUCTION

—〰—

What is a Godly Man? One hears words of encouragement to become a Godly man, or you hear women say, "Where can I find a Godly man?" I often wonder exactly what is the meaning of these phrases. We can assume everyone knows the answer to that question, but I wonder. Several years ago I received a call from a lady in Garland, Texas.

She was calling to see if I would present a program to the Women's Ministry at First Baptist Church in Garland. After asking the date and the usual questions concerning booking a program, I asked about the topic to be presented. She replied, "A Godly Man". To which I replied, "there ain't no such thing". Now I was teasing, but the reply threw the lady for a minute then she answered, "well, I don't know, that is just what they said." I quickly apologized for my poor attempt at a joke and told her I would be happy to come prepared to speak on "A Godly Man".

I am continually amused at God's timing. I had been working on a study of the men in the Bible. I had tentatively titled it "A Portrait of a Godly Man". I thought my motivation was to encourage deeper Bible study in the class of Single Adults I was leading in a Bible study time on Sunday mornings. My premise was to compose a rhyme with just enough information to peak the interest of the readers and then give the scripture reference for the "rest of the story". While I was working on this project, one of our Single ladies, who was a new Christian, called and ask if she could read the book I was writing. This took me aback because I was writing a book but no one knew that but me. I ask how she knew I was writing a book and she replied, God told me.

Now we all know what that phrase conjures up in the average person's mind. I agreed to let her read the manuscript and she promptly returned it to me stating that she thought it was a good book, but that it was not the one God told her to illustrate so could she read the other one. I told her there was not another one and she replied, "Don't play games with me. God would not have told me to illustrate your book unless there was one. I then remembered the men in the Bible project and tried to explain that to her. She broke in and said, "Would you meet me for lunch today?" More than a little baffled, I agreed. When I drove up to the restaurant, my friend was standing outside and asked me to come to her car before we went in to eat. I followed her to her car and she opened the back door and pulled out ten portraits of men. She said, "Who are these men?"

You see, she had not grown up in the church and did not have the "pictures" from church literature of artist's renditions of the men in the Bible. She had drawn, according to her, what God showed her. The scary thing is I recognized the men. We then went in to eat lunch and talk about this unusual situation. As we finished lunch, she handed me the check and told me to pay the bill since it looked like God had just put us in business. I did and after that as I would write a rhyme, she would pick it up and sketch her vision of what that man might have looked like. The result of her work is a wonderful gallery of framed 16x20 pencil sketches of the men and women in the Bible that now covers the walls of the third floor of FBC, Tyler's education building. It is a favorite spot for church members and visitors alike. The portraits are unique and portray characteristics of the individuals' stories through their facial expressions. They are wonderful gifts to all who view them. We never got around to putting the "book" into print and the portraits have never been reduced to a book size until now, but this book is the "rest of the story."

Karan Wynn Warr is the lady's name and she finished the portraits of the men just in time for the Garland Conference. She asked to attend the conference incognito, so to speak, so she could see the reactions to the portraits without people knowing she was the artist. We took forty portraits of the men in the Bible, unlabeled and hung them in the gathering area at FBC, Garland. As the ladies arrived they were told to pick a man...they could have any man they wanted. The portraits were numbered and the ladies chose their man and registered their choice with the number. This became the mixer for the day. The ladies had a great fun time. Upon beginning the conference, women were asked to tell us which man they chose and why. The results were very interesting. Ninety percent of the women chose Satan. Upon learning whom they had chosen, they were aghast! I assured them that he had knocked on all our doors and we had all let him in. The explanation as to why they chose that man was very revealing. Their reasons were: "He is not so good looking that some other woman will take him away from me"; "He looks friendly"; "There is just something about his smile".

The next favorite was the Apostle John. Reasons for choosing John were: "His eyes...he looks like he knows a secret." No one chose Jesus! One lady chose Adam, who, of course, was naked with a perfect body. Her reason for choosing him was, "he had such nice eyes". No one believed her! The interesting thing about Adam that most people miss is that he had no navel because he was not born of woman.

The search for a Godly man turned into a realization that most women don't really want a Godly man. They want one who will be Godly when and where the woman chooses. You know, go to church when she wants, put her first and etc. We discovered that since a Godly man would put God ahead of all else, most women would not be too happy with all the time he spent away from them. He would be out and about doing God's work when they wanted to go to the movies or wanted the yard mowed. We also learned that each individual needs to be concerned about his or her own Godliness and the end result will bring them the contentment they seek and only a Godly Woman could live with a Godly man! After all there really is no such thing…just men and women seeking to be all God wants them to be. No one really arrives until we are glorified with our Lord.

These portraits have traveled all over to conferences and been a true blessing in many people's lives. These portraits have been reproduced and can be enjoyed in this book. This gives you a little of the story behind the book and the interesting way that God works in our lives. Karan Wynn Warr has become one of my very best friends and co-laborers together for our Lord. She has also illustrated another one of my books titled "Whoa Man! See What God Did With A Rib!" This book is about the women in the Bible. Wynn is truly a giant in God's kingdom. It is to her I dedicate this book now titled, "A Godly Man? Who Can Find One?" I pray you will enjoy the search as you become more intimately acquainted with the candidates presented and will be motivated to look at your own portrait in the mirror we call Jesus.

THE TRINITY

The Spirit moved, God spoke,
And then the Light broke.
It took just seven days
To put everything in it's place.

God, The Father, The Spirit and The Son;
One in three and three in one.
They said in the beginning
Let's make man in our own image..

From the start until the end
The Three work among men;
To create, equip, love and guide,
Ever there by our side.

God the Father saw our need;
Then Jesus came to intercede.
When He had the victory won,
The Holy Spirit came to lean upon.

When comes the end of day,
T'will be the time to pay.
Judgment for the bad, the good,
Will your name be in His book?

God will sit upon His throne,
The Spirit will set the tone,
Jesus will sit by God's side,
With a twinkle in His eye.

To greet all who have believed,
At the glorious banquet feast.
Then forever more we'll be home
With God the Father, the Spirit, and the Son.

LESSONS FROM THE TRINITY

The Holy Trinity is one of the most complicated ideas of the Christian faith. We have the idea of three separate deities who are one. There is God the Father, God, the Son, and God the Holy Spirit. It is the hand of God, the Father, reaching out to touch the hand of God, the Son, that bridges the gap that separates God and His creation that came about because of the disobedience of mankind. The Father reaches down to offer us forgiveness through His mercy and Grace, the Son Reaches up by offering Himself to justify our redemption through His blood and the Holy Spirit comes to dwell in us to comfort and guide us by holding His hand under us to support our position with the Father.

The concept of the Trinity is one we will not truly understand until we are transformed in the next life, but we accept it because we believe the truths set forth in God's Holy Word. We also accept it because as we come to belief we have personal encounters with each part of the Trinity.

The Trinity is also our ultimate example of Godliness. Each part of the Trinity teaches us different aspects of becoming Godly. We learn how to be a Godly Father by learning from God the Father's example. We then learn how to be a Godly Son in the same way. The Holy Spirit is our guide to being a Godly friend.

We can also learn that each of these areas of Godliness come together as one in an individual as we live on this earth. So in our desire to grow from justification to sanctification we need to spend more time with each part of the Holy Trinity until we reach the state of glorification.

We should spend time reaching down to others, holding them up to God and then coming alongside to encourage them as they in turn grow in faith. It is in this process that we become candidates for the "Godly Man of the Year Award!"

Now this is not a reward from man, but a "well done, thy good and faithful servant" from our Heavenly Father.

Striving for this "reward" is striving to become more like the Son...sacrificing, dying to self, obedient unto death, victorious in the resurrection and an example and witness to the Father, the Son and the Holy Spirit.

Let's look into the Portraits of men found in scripture to see who among them could be candidates for the "Godly Man of the Year Award".....First there is Adam.

GENESIS 1:26-5:5

ADAM

God's crowning glory in creation occurred
upon the sixth day,
He surveyed the situation, formed man
from a clump of clay.
God breathed His Spirit into man and gave him
the awesome task
Of naming every species in the land;
it seemed a lot to ask.

Then God gave Adam dominion and
a perfect place to dwell.
Which in my humble opinion,
should've made all things well.
God then caused him to slumber;
took a rib and gave a wife,
Said, "Increase your number then go
and have a perfect life."

Two things Adam could not do,
they both involved a tree,
A test to see if He'd be true to the Sovereign Deity.
Alas, temptation was too great,
Adam ate of the fruit
Offered up to him by his mate;
God's word he forsook.

God came in the cool of his day;
Adam hid and was ashamed.
He did not know what to say except to try
and shift the blame.
Man cannot hide from God for He
knows our every thought.
If upon sin's pathway we do trod,
God's wrath we will wrought.

Consequences are always sure when
we do something wrong.
Labor and death we now endure for Adam was not strong.
But before we judge too harshly this first mortal man,
Look into your life and see how closely
you follow God's plan.

LESSONS FROM ADAM

Have you ever wondered what it must have been like to be the first human...

to open your eyes and see all of God's creation with its magnificence, beauty, and space? Do you think Adam looked around and then back at himself and wondered...are there any more like me? What about his first assignment? Can you imagine being asked to name all the other species? Have you ever wondered how he learned to walk, talk, eat and all the everyday things of life. Did he come pre-programmed? Did he wonder or just accept. Do you think he asked God any questions?

We have all had a different experience in coming into this world. Someone has said that the desire for freedom is evident even in the birth process, the fighting to get out of the womb. But not Adam. We have been birthed and nurtured in love. We have been taught and had examples to follow, but not Adam...Adam just was! Why? Because he was not born of woman, he didn't even have a navel! But just like you and me, God had a plan for Adam. Adam became very excited at each new development, especially the creation of Eve. And how about getting to walk and talk with God in the late afternoon? It doesn't get any better than that! And isn't that how one gets to be Godly? Spending time with the one who thought we were to die for?

Perhaps a good lesson from the life of Adam for each of us is to wonder and question less and just accept what the goodness of God provides. Adam was content and obedient until temptation came. That, for the most part, is the same for all mankind. But temptation does come so let's look into Adams experience to see what we should do when it comes.

Of course, there is the obvious choice, which Adam did not make, and that is to not yield to the temptation, but when we do, we need to accept our part, not blame others, confess our sin, not hide from God, nor let our shame render us immobile. We need to repent and ask for forgiveness.

We, like, Adam also need to learn how to accept the consequences of our actions and move forward trusting in God's goodness and Grace, growing closer to Him through the adversities our choices bring our way.

Godly men sometimes need second chances to help them learn to be Godly and move forward in their relationship with God.

GENESIS 4:1-5:

CAIN, ABEL, AND SETH

Adam had three sons; ill came to all but one.
Cain's offering was rejected; while Abel's was accepted.
When anger filled Cain's heart,
his actions tore their world apart;
Because he could not have his own way,
Cain killed Abel on one day.

Abel's blood cried out to God from 'neath earth's cold sod.
Cain's sin could not be hid, He must pay for what he did.
"Oh, the price is far too high!" Cain was heard to cry.
But don't you be shocked; God will not be mocked.

So the human race was left up to Adam's last son, Seth.
For righteous Abel had been slain;
Doom befell the seed of Cain.
It was from Seth that Noah came to survive and start again;
To replenish all the earth, t'was the reason for his birth.

Five generations came between,
still God's plan can be seen.
His father Lamech gave his name;
it was from Methusalah he came.
Methuselah was Enoch's son; Enoch was the translated one.
The seventh from Adam did not die;
his walk with God is why.

To walk with God is this; your every thought is His,
Oh to have Enoch's faith in our God so great!
Then those who descend from us will neither fight nor fuss
For they will understand all about God's plan.

LESSONS FROM CAIN, ABEL AND SETH

Could there have ever been anymore atypical siblings than Cain, Abel and Seth. What is it that all the personality experts tell us about birth order? These brothers may have been the prototype for the volumes written on the subject.

Cain was the oldest and in his mind, his younger brother Abel was favored even by God. This mindset turned into jealousy, escalated into anger and was consummated by murder. To further complicate the situation Cain thought he could conceal his deed. When God approached inquiring about Abel...Cain uttered his ever-infamous remark... "Am I my brother's keeper?" Duh!

Cain had not learned that if you do what is right you will be accepted, but if you do what is wrong then sin is crouching at your door because it desires you and you must master it.

Then to add to his shame when God pronounced his punishment, Cain cried out "it is more than I can bear." A Godly man could never utter such a statement because He would remember how much our Savior bore in our place. Then Cain became a marked man, a restless wanderer on the earth. He ended up in the land of Nod, East of Eden and started his family.

Abel on the other hand brought before the Lord a more favorable offering so that even in death he was avenged by his blood crying out from the ground to the Lord. Abel even in his death became the first member of the Hall of Faith found in Hebrews 11 and has the distinction of being the first shepherd. He was also the first martyr for truth. Could he be considered a choice for The Godly Man of the Year Award?

Lessons to be learned from Cain and Abel are that God hears those who come to him and he recognizes the innocent and the guilty and metes out justice to each. Each brother knew what God required; Cain chose to disregard that expectation while Abel obeyed. Knowing what God requires is not enough to make us Godly. Godliness is in the obedience.

The Bible is full of God's general guidelines and expectations for our lives. It is also full of more specific directions. Like Abel, we must obey regardless of the cost and trust God to make things right. What we offer to God must be from the heart – the best we are and have. We can also learn that the consequences of sin may last a lifetime.

Cain lived, but to his sorrow. Abel died to be memorialized for his faith. Favor with God is not earned or bargained for...favor with God is according to His Grace. Both Cain and Abel were recipients of God' Grace.

Seth, the third son of Adam, was the son born in his father's likeness, his image. Seth lived for 105 years before he became the father of Enoch and 807 years after. He also had other sons and daughters and thus became the one to add to the progeny of Adam.

We can learn from Seth and the genealogies that follow after his name that people are important to God as individuals, not just as races or nations. God refers to people by name, mentions their life span and descendants so the next time you feel overwhelmed in a vast crowd, remember that the focus of God's attention and love is on the individual and on you. All human beings are related, going back to Adam. Mankind is a family that shares one flesh and blood. When prejudice enters your mind or hatred invades your feelings remember we are all one big family. We are all a part of the family of God and He values each person as a unique creation of God. And yes, to be a Godly man one must remember that we are our brother's keeper.

GENESIS 5:29-10:32

NOAH (Rest)

"Noah! You are a foolish man, attempting such a silly plan.
Are you sure you heard from God,
or, perhaps, had too much nog?"
The people pointed and made fun,
but Noah just continued on.
He worked hard and built the ark
like God had said from the start.

Then he took them in two by two, the bird,
the cat, and the ewe.
Two of every species on this earth filled
the ark's heighth and girth.
Relentless rain began to pour just as Noah shut the door.
The scoffers then began to shake as their fear
did reverberate.

continued

They begged, but it was too late,
for God alone had set the date.
Forty days and nights it came, judgment in the form of rain.
'Til God said; "Send out a dove that won't
returned covered with mud,
But will carry a twig within its beak from
a tree on the mountain's peak.

Mount Ararat was the place,
Noah headed up the human race.
He built an altar upon the sod,
to sacrifice and worship God.
God had let them start anew;
He will do the same for me and you.
If you're tempted from God to part,
just stop and remember the ark!

While God has promised never again would
a flood punish man for sin,
He gave the rainbow as a sign,
to trust His word for all time.
His word came fresh and anew,
when Jesus died for me and you.
Belief in His Son is the only way,
to be safe on next judgment day.

Else you like Noah may fall when you
receive temptation's call.
T'was delight in another's sin brought a curse
to his son Ham.
Ham who sinned as a son, felt the pain in his loved ones.
To go against God's will can only bring winds of ill.

LESSONS FROM NOAH

Noah lived in a time when evil was so prevalent that he was the only man who could be found by God to be righteous, blameless and faithful to walk with God. Whoa, sounds like a candidate for the "Godly Man of the Year Award"!! So God gave him a project....take 120 years and build a boat. And he didn't just have to build any old boat. It had to be to God's specifications and then filled with two of every living creature on the earth! For Noah this meant a long-term commitment to a project. Not to mention patience, consistency and obedience. Now there is a lesson for us! Do you think Noah was a Godly man? Sounds good so far but…what about his bad days…you know when he got drunk and embarrassed himself in front of his sons? Have you ever noticed how soon we forget the good when we find something not so good to focus on? Could we not give the man a break considering his age, what he had just been through for the previous forty days and nights while the earth was being destroyed by a flood? Not to mention being locked up that long with his family. Probably one of the hardest places on earth to be Godly is with family.

Being Godly does not mean never making a mistake. Being Godly means striving to be God-like in obedience. That obedience is the long-term commitment. It means getting past your mistake and back on track with God. It means asking God for second, third and 40th chances. God wants us to commit to an entire lifetime of obedience and gratitude in response to our acceptance of God's grace.

Sometimes we can get full of ourselves and begin to think more of ourselves than we ought. We need to remember that even though we may have a good record of faithfulness, our sinful nature always travels with us. There will be bad days. There will be bad experiences. There will be bad choices. God does not always protect us from trouble or the consequences of our choices. But He cares for us in and through them. He gives the multiple chances because He loves us and sees in us the potential He placed in us.

Noah's epitaph can be found in Genesis 6:22 "Noah did everything just as God commanded him." Now that's a Godly Man!

GENESIS 10:8-11:8

NIMROD

Nimrod, Noah's great grandson,
Foreshadows the Evil one,
Because he desired a name,
The world was ne'er the same.

He chose to make himself a king
And strove all people to bring
Into the city called Babel;
Obedience to God began to unravel.

He built a tower to reach into heaven;
His plans were filled with leaven.
For into the world he would not go
Self pride was what made him glow.

continued

So the city was renamed;
Following Nimrod was to blame.
No longer called the gate of God,
Its people were scattered abroad.

God did their speech confound
Confusion was forever to abound.
Once again all were guilty of sin,
Therefore did God intervene.

So now we have different nations,
Different places, different stations.
The tower was destroyed by God
That had been built by Nimrod.

God's mercy had twice came
And now He turned to Abram;
For Adam and Noah's kin
Had greatly disappointed Him.

LESSONS FROM NIMROD

Nimrod, now there is a name for you! It doesn't take a genius to know that someone named Nimrod probably was not a candidate for "Godly Man of the Year"! But Nimrod was the grandson of Noah. Don't you know he had a problem with always being compared to such a man? He was also a mighty warrior and hunter. As is the case with some people who have great gifts, pride became a problem for Nimrod. He is considered by some to be the founder of the great, godless Babylonian empire. He was a part of a group who said, "Come, let us build ourselves a city with a tower that reaches to the heavens, so that we may make a name for ourselves and not be scattered over the face of the whole earth." One has to wonder, if on some level, he was trying to live up to grandpa.

But, the Lord. Is there anymore powerful phrase? God confounded their language and scattered them over the face of the whole earth. They were building a tower called Babel as a monument to their own greatness, something for the whole world to see. It was a great human achievement, but it was not a monument to God. Two generations and the attribute of Godliness seems to have been lost. Not only that but his tower came tumbling down and rather than their name being scattered over the face of the whole earth, the people themselves were scattered and began speaking in different languages. One of the things about speaking in different languages is that not everyone understands which leads to the loss of communication. Then with the loss of communication comes greater miss-understanding, fear, and strife.

Suffice it to say, Nimrod was probably not a good candidate for the Godly Man of the Year Award. We learn from Nimrod that the only towers and monuments that we should erect are those to God's glory. When we place monuments to edify ourselves, we can count on there being a "but, the

Lord". We also need to remember that we are not judged on our human family tree, but rather on our relationship to our Heavenly Father. Heard of any kids named Nimrod? Today the name is used as a derogatory term if used at all.

GENESIS 11_25

FATHER ABRAHAM (Exalted Father)

Man of Faith, Father Abraham,
Titles we give to a mortal man,
Who learned to walk along with God
Across some pretty shaky sod.

God said, "Leave your home and your kin,
Start anew; begin all over again.
Travel far and without delay,
Trust in me to know the way.

But, every now and again,
Life was hard for Abraham,
He would try and take the lead
Forgetting God's help to seek.

God would take him by the hand,
Draw him close once again;
Until at last he truly knew
All God's promises do come true.

Two women bore him sons,
Only Sarah's was the promised one.
Then God put him to the test
To see whom he loved best.

Abraham had learned his part.
He gave God his whole heart.
Jehovah Jireh did provide
That day t'was a ram that died.

For Isaac was to be the one
God would build His nation on.
The nation which in God's plan
Would share His love with every man.

"Man of Faith" – we now say,
But remember, faith came day by day.
He who started and sometimes stumbled
Grew great only as he was humbled.

Can you say with Father Abraham;
"I can't, but I know God can?"
Don't be discouraged nor despair,
Keep on trusting, because God IS There!

LESSONS FROM ABRAHAM

Abraham was a man who came to a fork in the road... one possibility was to stay where he was and be in control of his future, the other was to depend totally on God and take his entire family and just set out for parts unknown. It's easy to see what choice a Godly man would make, but think what faith is required to follow with no plan in place. This is probably the greatest obstacle for Godliness today. We have been saturated with the self-made man image.

We know that the road that looks like we are in control, in truth, is not really an option, because we just like to think we have control. We have control of the choices we make, but not the consequences. God desires dependence, trust and faith in him, not faith in our own abilities. All are requirements for Godliness.

Abraham was a Godly man. His faith pleased God. He became the founder of the Jewish nation. He was respected by others and was courageous in defending his family at any cost, well, most of the time. He was a loving husband, father and friend. He was a successful and wealthy rancher...but... and there always seems to be a but... Abraham did not do well under pressure as can be seen in the distortions of truth that surfaced when he felt his life was in danger concerning his wife. Sarai was a beautiful woman and as they traveled in unfamiliar territory Abraham was willing to share her with other men in order to insure his safety. On more than one occasion, he passed Sarai off as his sister rather than his wife. But, and we see here that all buts are not bad. In this instance, as Abraham spent more time with God, he learned from experience that God is faithful so he was ready and willing when God told him to sacrifice his son, Isaac. God was faithful and provided a sacrifice just in the nick of time. One can only imagine what was going through Abraham's emotions as he prepared to sacrifice his promised son. We surely can learn from his experience to trust in God's faith-fulness even when we cannot see or understand His will.

Abraham's Godly qualities were always there but grew as he walked with God day by day. He sometimes stumbled, but God knew his heart. We can learn from Abraham to humble ourselves, pray, spend time with God and then remember all God has done for us in the past to gain strength for each new day. We can also learn to live in the moment trusting God for the future He has planned for us. That surely is a trait for a Godly man.

GENESIS 25:19-28:9

ISAAC (Laughter)

Abraham and Sarah had no heir,
then God said to get prepared.
When their promised son came
they chose Isaac for his name.
He was a kind and gentle son;
the kind you can depend upon.
He helped his father on that day,
built an altar without delay.

Isaac, 'tho busy with the task stopped
just once a question to ask.
"Where is the sacrificial lamb?"
But his father just looked down.
Then with the time was right,
Isaac's hands were bound tight.
His body laid upon the wood
while o'er him his father stood.

37

The knife was held high. It seemed death was nigh.
Then God spoke and said, "NO!"
Their faith withheld the blow.
God provided a ram to pay on that very special day.
Twelve years later Sarah died, now Abraham must decide.

He sought for Isaac a wife to comfort and
help him in his life.
Isaac again was content when Rebecca shared his tent.
Years passed without a seed.
They talked with God about their need.
How they longed for a son;
they received two instead of one.

Isaac served his God well with a faith —words can't tell.
The commitment he had to keep,
like his wells—it ran deep.
When he was old, blind and near death,
deception upon him crept.
It came from those he loved;
how they lied, pushed and shoved.

Blessings he gave to both his sons,
knowing Jacob was the chosen one.
But he knew within his heart, all was well –
he could now depart.
For God is in control of more than just our mortal soul.
He who made us everyone will still be
God when day is done.

LESSONS FROM ISAAC

Being "special" does not make one Godly. Godliness comes from being God centered, not self-centered. Too often, we as humans, attribute specialness onto others to their detriment. A big mistake is to believe your press. That is true whether your "press" is good or bad. Isaac is a case in point. Isaac was an only child...he was special, especially to his parents who had waited a long time for the promised son. His very name means laughter, which makes it ironic since both of his parents laughed when God told them they would conceive a child in their old age. He was also special because he was the chosen one sent from God. Amidst all that specialness life was not always special for Isaac. But then life is not always what it seems...the grass is not always greener. In fact, Columnist Erma Bombeck says "it is only greener over the septic tank."...so what looked like an ideal family situation was anything but because of the desire to blend families. Father Abraham wanted to have his cake and eat it too which always leads to trouble. Because of his love for his son, Ishmael, born to Sarah's handmaid Rahab, Abraham was blinded to God's plan concerning Isaac. The result was a family split by jealousy.

To Isaac's credit he grew up strong and free of violent passions. Now we're talking Godly! He had a quiet, gentle nature. Isaac was dutiful, dependable, patient and faithful. He lived up to his name and was a joy. He lived the longest of the three patriarchs and traveled the least. He also had the fewest extraordinary adventures unless you count being offered up as a sacrifice by your father. That seems to be pretty extraordinary to me. But even in that situation, Isaac showed Godly characteristics. He trusted his father. To be Godly we also need to trust our Father even to the death.

Isaac was a good family man and father. He had his priorities in the right place. He lived to the ripe old age of

180. He died at Maure. He is remembered for keeping his commitments because that is what Godly men do. Isaac is a good candidate for the "Godly Man of the Year Award".

The lessons for Godliness we can learn from Isaac are first, that patience brings rewards. Second we learn that God's plans and promises are larger than people and God keeps His promises in spite of our unfaithfulness. Third, we can learn how playing favorites and deceit only bring conflict and pain. Anyone desiring to be a Godly would do well to follow the good example found in the life of Isaac.

GENESIS 25-36

ESAU (Hairy)

Esau was rough, red and hairy.
Must have looked a little scary.
He loved the world and his bow;
Always a hunting he would go.

The pleasure of the chase
For Esau took first place
His appetite for the game
Soon brought him to shame.

He traded his birthright for some stew;
T'was a foolish thing to do;
Yet, Esau never seemed to learn;
We cannot have all for which we yearn.

His choices all had one connection
They all led in the wrong direction.
What he could not accept at all
Was the part he played in every fall.

He asked his father for a second chance;
Took a blessing without a second glance.
From Esau to Edom his name was changed,
His home became the mountain range.

When God's ways we don't understand,
Accept only He knows the inner man.
That is why when we are stressed,
It's wise to trust God knows best.

LESSONS FROM ESAU

Looking for a Godly man? Look elsewhere…this man is a man's man! Whatever that is! Esau was born a fraternal twin. From the beginning he loved adventure..excitement. He never thought about tomorrow or the consequences one's choices bring. He had the "if it feels good do it" frame of mind. He was always living for the present moment with no thought of tomorrow. He married at the age of 40 taking two Hittite wives. Later he married two Ishmaelite women, became the servant of his brother and was eventually banished from the family. His name was changed from Esau meaning hairy to Edom to remind him and all who knew him of the consequences that come from bad choices. Do you ever wonder what Esau could have been if he had desired to be a Godly man over being a man's man? We need to be careful when choosing our mentor in life. We need to be careful for what we pray…we may just get it to our sorrow.

The lessons we can learn from Esau are that God allows certain events for His over all purpose, but we still have a choice and are responsible for our actions and the consequences these actions bring. We need to remember that consequences are important things to consider. They are always life-changing.

Esau is not remembered as a Godly man even though he apparently was able to forgive the rejection from his mother and the deception of his brother. Even though we may forgive it cannot always mend the relationships. No one can deny that Esau did not get a fair shake from his family, but he does have to be held responsible for allowing his appetite to cloud his good sense.

Esau was more interested in appeasing his appetites than he was in preserving his birthright. As the first born, the birthright should have been his, and even though he was deceived by his mother and brother, that does not excuse his willingness to sell his birthright for stew! We also need to remember sometimes there is not an opportunity for a second chance. Life also has a ripple effect...choices we make change others lives as well as our own.

To be a Godly man is to hang on to our birthright...that is our relationship to our Heavenly Father. Too often, we like Esau, are willing to sell out to our sorrow.

GENESIS 25-50

JACOB (Supplanted)

Jacob was an important man.
The third link in God's plan;
Not a perfect hero you see,
but a whole lot like you and me.
Jacob was also a gentle man,
easily swayed by a woman's hand.
First his mom and then his wife
took control of Jacob's life.

Jacob tricked his father with the help of his mother;
And received the blessing causing quite a stink!
Jacob left home to seek a wife,
but also – for fear of his life.
Deception was a family trait;
Jacob discovered way too late.

Jacob worked for seven years to wed
the girl he loved so dear.
But Uncle Laban had other plans he
gave Jacob Leah's hand.
Jacob was not one to pale.
He worked seven more for Rachel.
His children numbered twelve.
They become the tribes of Israel.

Jacob knew of God's schemes.
It was revealed to him in dreams.
Once he saw God and a ladder;
awakened and built an altar.
Jacob wrestled all one night;
thought t'was a man he did fight.
But it was God who blest him there
and changed his name to Israel.

God touched his hip in a special place.
It changed the look upon his face.
With a limp he now did walk to remind him of God's talk.
The story of his life is in his names.
Jacob meant trickster, player of games.
While Israel was a soldier of God marching
thru earth's thick fog.

LESSONS FROM JACOB

Jacob was the fraternal twin of Esau. His name means supplanter. It is said that as his brother was being born, Jacob grabbed on to his heel in an attempt to supplant the birth order. That became the theme of his life...using treachery to displace, uproot, overthrow, replace and undermine his brother. How can this be a candidate for "Godly Man of the Year"? But, as is the usual case, one gets back double what they give out to others. While eventually Jacob was successful in obtaining the special blessing from his father payback time came from Uncle Laban. Jacob is remembered for his determination and his good business acumen. He is also known for relying on his own resources, accumulating wealth for its own sake and being easily manipulated. The old adage we reap what we sow was certainly true for Jacob. God had some work to do before Jacob became Godly.

On the plus side we see where Jacob was a hard worker and loved deeply. But he was easily swayed by a woman's touch. This is evident in his relationship to his mother and his wives. First he was wed to Leah, who bore him ten sons. Rachel was his second wife and she bore him two sons. These sons make up the twelve tribes of Israel. There were other children from Leah and the two wives handmaids. Still not much evidence of Godliness until he had a dream in which God revealed the details of His plans to Jacob. Upon awakening from this dream Jacob built an altar and then wrestled all night with God. Then God blessed him there and changed his name from Jacob, meaning supplanter and trickster, to Israel which means soldier of God. God also left him with a reminder of their conversation in the form of a limp. When someone comments, "What's in a name?" it might be wise to look at the life of Jacob. He lived up to both of his names. But once he grabbed on to God, God grabbed onto him and life was never the same. What is your name? When others hear your name do they see someone who has grabbed on to God? That is on attribute of Godliness. Or perhaps you are still wrestling with God.

Lessons Jacob learned are that security does not lie in the accumulation of goods…security lies in trusting God. Have you learned that lesson yet? We can also see through Jacob's life that God has a plan for each life and even when we stray from that plan, our God is able to weave our actions into His ultimate plan. Another lesson to be learned is that our significance is not based upon our personal character, but on the very character of God. Under the name of Jacob, we don't see a Godly man, but once God changes things we see Israel as one of God's godliest men. It is comforting to know that God doesn't look for perfect men to find a Godly man. He looks for one who will grab hold of Him.

GENESIS 30-50

JOSEPH (May God Add)

It was a coat of many colors that hackled Joseph's brothers.
They were in such a snit, Joseph found himself in a pit.
Then along came some travelers,
a band of merchants and some hagglers.
Joseph's brothers did not think twice,
they sold Joseph for a price.

The coat once upon his back was left to seal the pact.
When Jacob sought for his son he feared
the worst was done.
While his father cried and mourned,
Joseph's life took another turn.
For he was sold once again to one of the Egyptians.

continued

Potiphar was now in charge of Joseph's life, by and large.
But Joseph met each new strife;
even withstood Potiphar's wife.
Joseph was blessed with confidence
and a lot of plain common sense.
When trials came he asked not why,
he just sought a plan to try.

Soon he was a slave no more for God
had opened up a door.
He became a ruler in the land; famine came,
but Joseph had a plan.
He saw God in others dreams;
helped them understand things.
He was there in their hour of need to show
the folly of their greed.

Joseph had a heart of love,
forgave his brothers with a hug.
The apple of his father's eye did in the land of Egypt die.
His brothers a promise made as Joseph assured God's aid.
When the family left for home,
they were to take Joseph's bones.

Joseph's life foreshadowed Christ,
not just once or even twice.
In more than one hundred ways
future things God displayed.
We can learn how to live if we some thought
to Joseph give.
If things don't go the way they should,
trust in God to bring the good.

LESSONS FROM JOSEPH

We all know the story of Joseph and his coat of many colors. But there is so much more. In looking at Joseph's life, he sometimes appears to have been a little naïve. He seemed to always think the best of everyone and every situation. The sharing of his dream with his brothers and the trusting of his prison cell mate shows evidence of at least in-experience. But the same examples can be evidence of an open heart. Open hearts are necessary if we are to become Godly.

Joseph was the first-born son of Jacob and Rachel. He had ten half brothers through his Aunt Leah. So his birth was not a happy occasion for most of the family. The fact that his father always appeared to love him best did not help his situation in the family. This made life at home a little hard, but in retrospect, God was using Joseph's circumstances to get Joseph to the position God had planned. God always uses our circumstances to direct our paths. It was his open heart-edness that kept him strong through his time in the pit, in the slave market place, in his encounter with Potiphar's wife, through the rejection of Potiphar, in prison and then gave him the grace to become a strong leader in a strange land. Yes, God was in his heart and directing his steps.

Joseph was spiritually sensitive, had integrity, and gentleness. He was faithful. He also was magnanimous and had a forgiving spirit. Only a Godly man could have welcomed brothers who meant him harm with open arms. And yet, he was no longer naïve. His experiences had given him the wisdom to test the waters. He was full of self-assurance and wisdom. No matter what lemon life seemed to hand him, he knew how to make lemonade. Joseph did not spend a lot of time asking why me. He looked at each situation and said, "what shall I do".

Joseph is a type of Christ and as such is certainly one of scripture's most Godly men. His most famous quote is

"What you meant for evil God meant for good" found in Genesis 50:20. How much better life would be if we could learn the lessons from the life of Joseph. To learn life lessons from Joseph could mean the same type of epitaph for our life as was found to be true for Joseph. "Can we find any one like this man, one in whom is the Spirit of God?" Gen. 41:38 Now there is a definition of a Godly man...one in whom is the Spirit of God!

EXODUS-DEUTERONOMY

MOSES (Drawn out)

T'was in a basket on the Nile,
Pharoah's daughter found the child.
Took him home to be her own; gave him access to a throne.
Jocabed had saved her son from the decree of an evil one.
Miriam had watched her brother
'til he was safe with another.

Moses grew and gave great joy,
although he was another's boy.
The one who loved him best gave him suckle at her breast.
She taught him as he grew all about those called Hebrew.
This was according to God's plan
to free His people from this land.

continued

When things finally came to a head,
from the land of Egypt Moses fled.
Into the desert this man went;
took a wife – became content.
Until one day on his shepherd's job,
Moses heard the voice of God.
The burning bush was not consumed,
Holy Ground –He assumed.

When God made His request, Moses could but protest.
In the end Moses knew, whate'er God said he would do.
Moses agreed to go and got a rod to represent
the power of God.
It took ten plagues and even death before
Moses work could be blest.

The Pharoah said, "Take them all, the young,
the old, before I fall."
Then God thru Moses parted the Red Sea,
led God's people on to liberty.
When God's finger wrote the law
upon stone tablets, Moses saw.
When the people's faith stalled Moses sought
to avenge them all.

To keep others away from pain,
Moses requested his name,
Be stricken from God's Holy Book
when God's law they had forsook.
Moses led them for forty years through
a trail of many tears
As they traveled by the cloud until
at last they trusted God.

One last flash of foolish pride,
he could not then in Canaan abide.
Moses slipped and struck the rock,
but was clothed in heaven's frock.
And the God he loved and served offered
a reward so well deserved.
Moses got to take a look and see,
the Promised Land that was to be.

LESSONS FROM MOSES

Now Moses could be a great candidate for our "Godly Man of the Year Award". It took a while for him to realize God's plan for his life, but hey, he had a rocky beginning, literally! In fact, only God knows just how rocky it must have been to be an infant in a basket in the Nile River! Even Moses would not remember the experience. But, no matter how rocky life begins or for that matter gets from time to time. God does have a plan for every life. God was not surprised by the rocky beginning...he knew all the time and was going ahead to prepare Moses for the work he was to do.

Moses' life can be divided into three parts, each containing forty years. He spent 40 years living and learning all about Egyptian Pharaohs, then 40 years in the desert learning all about God, and then 40 years wandering in the wilderness learning about mankind before he accomplished his life's mission, getting God's people to the promised land. And then he didn't even get to go in...just got to take a look. Moses learned "it's not about me", big time.

We can learn a lot about being "Godly" from Moses. We can also learn a lot about God.

We can learn that God prepares us, even if it takes a while. He uses us, in spite of us. And God does his greatest work through frail people. God's timetable is not limited to a twenty-four hour day, His timetable is life-sized! We need to learn to wait upon the Lord. Too often we try and rush ahead thinking time's a'wastin. Moses knew all about this mind-set. We see this in his reaction to becoming aware of social injustice. No wonder God sent him into the desert. Moses needed to learn how to react correctly. He needed to be molded into the man God wanted him to be. We today, also need lessons in how to react. Could this be the reason God gave us all the intimate details in Moses' life?

Until Moses "grew up" spiritually he exhibited an inquis-
itive nature, did not always recognize the talents of others,
had bouts of anger and pride, but once he "grew up" he realized that he was commissioned by God and given the gift of
miracles and administration. He learned to be obedient and
to love God above all. In the end, isn't that what makes a
Godly man?

JOSHUA

JOSHUA (Salvation)

Joshua, who was the son of Nun,
Is the one Moses depended upon.
When the Promised Land caught his eye,
He sent men with Joshua to spy.

Ten came back all afraid.
Caleb and Joshua were set to stay.
When others of giants told,
Joshua assured honey flowed.

Fear kept them from their home,
So for forty years they did roam.
Of those who left on that day,
Only Joshua and Caleb got to say;

"Here we are again, let's go on in,
We've paid enough for others sin."
They circled Jericho and gave a yell,
Then watched as the walls fell.

Joshua learned at Moses' feet,
God's advice can't be beat.
A mighty warrior he became
As he led Israel home again.

With conquering kings no more a task,
Joshua did all that God ask;
He divided the land into lots,
Every tribe received a plot.

Joshua died at a hundred and ten.
He was buried in the Promised land.
But greater still than his nerve
Is the awesome God he served.

LESSONS FROM JOSHUA

Joshua could just be the best candidate so far. Joshua is one of those men with whom no one could find fault. He just always did the right thing. Joshua followed the Lord whole-heartedly. Moses saw in Joshua, great potential. He appointed Joshua to the position of commander only two months after the Exodus from Egypt. He became Moses Successor and is the one who finally got to lead the Israelites into the Promised Land. This Godly man was a master in military strategy. Military giants down through the ages have gone back and studied the strategy techniques of Joshua. Of course, we know that Joshua's strategies came from God. When God directed, Joshua was committed to those directions no matter how illogical they might have appeared to others. A case in point is the battle plan for taking the city of Jericho.

Most military leaders would have been insulted with the direction to march around the city seven times with the priests blowing their trumpets and then on the seventh day to march around seven times still blowing the trumpets and on the seventh time for all the people to give a shout. But even more difficult than that was the instruction not to say anything. Joshua must have been a well-respected leader for his followers to have obeyed. But, then again, they had a long experience with this Godly man and knew where he got his instructions. They had also witnessed his faith, his energy and his relationship with God. They had seen the results of their fathers choosing to follow the advice of the ten spies rather than accepting the words of Caleb and Joshua. They knew that Caleb and Joshua were the only two who survived from the Exodus to enter into the Promised Land.

Even at the end of his life, Joshua was sharing with others the benefits of being Godly. He reminded them of all God had done for them. He instructed them as to what they should do and then he proclaimed, " Choose this day whom you will serve, but as for me and my house, we will serve the Lord!" A Godly man always takes a stand and is not swayed by the decisions of others because he is in touch with God and is always listening to the still small voice of God, remembering past experiences, trusting in God's mercy and grace. Yes, Joshua looks like a good candidate for the Godly Man of the Year Award! We can learn the way to Godliness from Joshua. Always follow God's lead!

JUDGES; I SAMUEL

JUDGES

The people had claims and held grudges,
So Moses set up a system of judges.
One for each of twelve tribes,
On them justice would ride.

There was Othneil, Ebed and Shambar,
Gideon, Barah and Deborah.
They served from Joshua to Saul
Seeking God's best for all.

Abimelech, Tola, Jair and Japheth
Helped remind God is over all.
Ibzan, Elon and Abdon
Held court until Samson.

When Samson lost his hair,
T'was Delilah who was there.
But God returned his power;
Allowed him to have his hour.

After an interim Eli came,
He the first prophet trained.
Samuel finished up their work
Even tho they had lost the Ark.

Judges by the nation were rejected
A king was now expected
Desire for what others have got
Infested the whole of the lot.

But t'was during this time
God provided for the line
Thru the union of Boaz and Ruth
Came the Savior, The Truth.

LESSONS FROM THE JUDGES

There were twelve judges, one for each tribe but only eleven were candidates for a Godly Man. Two of the judges, Deborah and Othniel were leaders of the nation. Gideon is remembered as one who delivers. Shamgar and Ibzan were local heroes. Tola was at mediator and administrator. Ehud and Jair provided rest and peace. Elon and Abdon were hard working yet unsung while Samson is the most famous and powerful. Jephthat was a rude, petty dictator.

This synopsis tells us that each had strengths and weaknesses. We can learn that great strength in one area does not make up for great weaknesses in other areas. We can also learn that God's presence does not overwhelm a person's personal will. But the greatest lesson of all is that God can and does use us in spite of our weaknesses. God chooses leaders by his standards, not ours. But wise leaders also choose good helpers.

Lets look at some facts about these judges:

First was Othniel who judged for 40 years. He is most remembered because he captured a powerful Canaanite city

Second was Ehud who judged for 80 years. He is remembered for killing Eglon and defeating the Moabites

Third was Shamgar whose time of judging is unrecorded but we do know he killed 600 Philistines with an ox goad.

Fourth was Deborah with Barak who served 40 years. She is remembered for defeating Sisera and the Canaanites and later sang a victory song with Barak about the Lord going forth before me.

Fifth was Gideon who also served 40 years and we know that he destroyed his family idols, used a fleece to determine God's will, raised an army of 10,000 and defeated 135,000 Midianites with only 300 soldiers.

Sixth was Tola who judged Israel for 23 years

Seventh was Jair who served for 22 years and had 30 sons!

Eighth was Jephthah who served 6 years and is remembered for making a rash vow, defeating the Ammonites, and for battling jealous Ephraim

Ninth was Ibzan who served 7 years and is known to have had 30 sons and 30 daughters.

Tenth was Elon who judged 10 years and that is all that is recorded of his judgeship

Eleventh was Abdon who judged for 8 years. He had 40 sons and 30 grandsons, each of whom had his own donkey

Twelfth was Samson who judged for 20 years. We know that he was a Nazirite, killed a lion with his bare hands, burned the Philistine wheat fields, killed 1,000 Philistines with the jawbone of an ass, tore off an iron gate, was betrayed by Delilah and destroyed thousands of Philistines in one last mighty act.

But perhaps the best questions to ask here is "For what will you be remembered?" We need to keep a close reign on our resumes if we want to be remembered as Godly.

I SAMUEL 9-31

SAUL (Asked of God)

When the people desired a king
It caused God a sorrowing.
For He should have been the one
They bowed to and counted on.

God gave in to their request;
Told Samuel that Saul was best.
But the prophet, before he died,
Shamed the people for their pride.

Saul was a tall and striking man,
Just the one for God's plan.
God chose him to be a king,
Then took him beneath his wing.

continued

And tho Saul looked the part,
Things were different in his heart.
He had skills, talents – useful tools,
When on allows God to rule.

Oft times the choices Saul made
Were what led to his decay.
The Lord was often grieved
Because His words were not received.

So while Saul was still enthroned
God chose another for His own.
He gave Samuel the task again,
To anoint still another man.

When King Saul heard of this
He grew angry-clenched his fist;
Felt he knew just what to do.
He would young David pursue.

As Saul lived by the sword,
By his own he was gored.
But this did not forestall
Being nailed upon a wall.

A sad end for Saul indeed,
He followed not God's creed.
A lesson too for you and me,
Be all God wants you to be!

LESSONS FROM SAUL

Saul, the son of Kish and a descendant of Benjamin had a humble beginning. In fact, he was out looking for a lost donkey when he met up with Samuel. He was referred to as "rif raff" (a farmer) at his confirmation at Mizpah. He even hid among the baggage. Perhaps this is why he so often listened to the voice of his own insecurity. What looked like a good beginning for a candidate for the Godly Man of the Year Award ended with the pride that precedes a fall.

Saul was courageous and generous.

He was also insecure, jealous, and religious.

He became disobedient, deceitful and impulsive.

He failed to learn the lesson that God wants obedience from the heart not mere acts of religious ritual.

He never learned that obedience involves sacrifice.

But one needs to also remember that sacrifice is not always obedience.

Saul began to feel full of himself. He presumed to make an offering himself rather than waiting for Samuel before going into battle. He never learned that God has different places for each of us to serve. We need to tend to our task rather than deciding to take on the tasks God has assigned to others. Sometimes power turns our windows of opportunity into mirrors in which we drown on too much of self. A lesson to be learned from Saul's weaknesses is they can help us remember our need for God's guidance and help.

Perhaps the greatest lesson to learn from Saul is when we reject God...He will reject us.

I SAMUEL 16-I KINGS 2

DAVID (Beloved)

David was but a lad when he slew the giant bad.
With a sling and a rock, it took him but one shot.
A mighty warrior he became.
The women sang out his name.
Then upon King Saul's death he rose to fame and wealth.

This humble shepherd boy felt the wonder of God's joy.
He was chosen to be the king, with a very special blessing.
T'was to be from his line the Savior would come in time.
He was a man from God's own heart;
seemed to have a perfect start.

continued

Yet, he was a mortal man who often failed God's plan.
Pride o'er took his life, when he took another's wife.
Then to cover this foul deed,
he helped another death to meet.
When he thought t'was safe again,
God revealed his wicked sin.

The punishment he would pay, God allowed David to say.
And though his heart was grieved,
sin's consequences he received.
Tho David sinned many times, he repented of his crimes.
And because he could confess,
He received God's forgiveness.

This gave such joy within his soul,
he wrote psalms that now do show;
God is faithful, just and true, where'er we are,
he'll see us thru.
David knew this on the day he did
a charge to Solomon say;
"Be strong and show yourself a man,
Be still and know God can."

LESSONS FROM DAVID

It has been said of David that he was God's kind of king, a man after God's own heart, but exactly what does that mean? Let's see on the "good" side, David was kind, benevolent, forgiving, repentant, courageous and generally at peace with God. He was the greatest king of Israel, an ancestor of Jesus Christ, and is listed in the Hall of Faith found in Hebrews 11. On the other hand, David was also a betrayer, a liar, an adulterer, disobedient, a poor parent and a murderer. We also know that David was a shepherd, a musician, poet, soldier, husband, father, son, friend and king. So how can we possibly reconcile these traits and find a candidate for a Godly Man? Could it be that he was human?

While it is the first list we admire, it is the second list with which we can identify. The second list could be true of almost all of us. It should give us comfort to recognize that God did not hide David's short comings, rather He had David's story recorded in His word "warts and all" for all to see and to teach us about the very nature of God and man.

To be a Godly man must mean one is to strive to be like God. In order to do this, one must first know God. To know God is more than just to have head knowledge about God. One must have an intimate personal relationship with God. David knew God. He had learned about God from his family, but he also had personal experiences with God. He understood what God meant when he talked about shepherding and sheep. It helped him to understand following and faith. David's experiences with God gave him and unchangeable belief in the faithful and forgiving nature of God. So that when he lived life with "gusto" and found himself knee-deep in sin, David knew that he must be quick to confess his sins. His confessions were more than lip service, they came from a repentant heart. Because of this David experienced the joy of forgiveness even though he had to suffer the consequences of his sins. David also learned not to repeat his sins, he learned from his mistakes. We might say he learned to stay and deal. In doing this he learned how to worship God as is evidenced in his history and his Psalms.

We can learn from David that we will stray from the fold, do dumb things, sin, but also recognize that the first step in dealing with our sins and mistakes is to admit them to ourselves and God honestly, without excuses or justifications. We can learn that even though we have to pay the consequences of our sins, we don't have to live laden down with guilt and shame. We can accept forgiveness from God and then go and do great things in God's kingdom. We can become Godly men who understand that God greatly desires our complete trust and worship. A Godly man remembers, I can't, but God can.

II SAMUEL 12:24- I KINGS 11:43

SOLOMON (Peaceable)

Bathsheba and David had a son,
They called him Solomon.
We remember his wealth, his wives,
And that he was terribly wise.

But a lad when he became a king
Wearing a robe, a crown, and a ring.
A temple he built unto the Lord
But failed to obey God's Holy Word.

The loyalty of his subjects he lost
By extracting too great of a cost.
The advice of his father he forgot;
Got caught up in a magician's art.

God forbade him to worship another.
He learned too late to recover.
So that when Solomon died,
His son inherited but one tribe.

Solomon reigned for forty years,
Amassed more wealth than his peers.
But great wisdom is of little use
If God's instruction you abuse.

Great palaces, a fling with a queen
Do not true happiness bring.
Consequences for what we have done
Is also something we pass on.

God's nation was soon divided
With God's judgment they collided.
For they followed evil kings,
Until Elijah came upon the scene.

LESSONS FROM SOLOMON

Two lessons to be learned from Solomon just jump right out at you. First, he disobeyed God and second he went against his father, King David's last words. We can learn how easy it is to know what is right and then not do it. Knowledge without obedience doesn't sound like wisdom and yet Solomon is remembered as the wisest man who ever lived. We must remember that knowledge is not necessarily wisdom. Wisdom is a gift from God. Knowledge is learned facts. One can be wise without an abundance of knowledge. Too often we equate wisdom with knowledge.

Solomon's strengths were his position as David's chosen heir, his building of God's Temple in Jerusalem, his accomplishments as a diplomat, trader, collector and patron of the arts.

Solomon's weaknesses and mistakes include his enjoyment of the privileges of his position without acknowledging the responsibilities. He tended to pursue the privileges to the neglect of the responsibilities. This led to alienating his own people while catering to foreign dignitaries. He overtaxed and over-worked his subjects to build himself up in the eyes of the world. Solomon also sealed agreements by marrying pagan women and then allowed his wives to affect his loyalty to God.

Solomon is a great example of how effective leadership can be of little use when one has an ineffective personal life. Solomon's frustrations can be found in his book, "The Songs of Solomon". His "songs" tell a sad story, but even sadder still is his book," Ecclesiastes", where we find life without God is lived in vain. Solomon learned the lesson of repentance too late. Actions speak louder than words.

Solomon had all the tools to be a Godly man. What he lacked was the heart. With Solomon it was all about me. Perhaps this is the greatest lesson we can learn if we want to be a candidate for a Godly man; life on this earth is not about me...it is about God! To be Godly one must live seeking God's face, His grace and His will. God must have first place. If we will spend all of eternity worshipping and praising God, don't you think this life is the dress rehearsal? Only Satan would have you believe it's all about the wine, the women and the song and how they relate to self. True wisdom tells you to seek God with all your heart and understanding.

I AND II KINGS
MATTHEW

ELIJAH

Elijah was a prophet man, sent to warn men of their sin.
He never forgot it was his job to proclaim,
"Jehovah alone is God".
He warned Ahab of the strife if he listened to his wife.
The nation would feel pain; God would withhold the rain.

The heat of Jezebel's wrath caused Elijah to find the path
That led beside a brook where he of God's bounty took.
When the brook had all dried up a widow
offered him a cup.
Elijah found her by the gate as she did upon death await.

continued

Elijah said to bake the bread until it rained
they would be fed.
Her son got sick and died, to which ole Elijah replied:
"God give this child breath; take from him
the stench of death."
The lad awoke and the widow knew t'was
Elijah's God who was true.

God told Elijah to go again back to where Ahab reigned.
War against Baal to prepare,
victory's fire came with prayer.
Again this did Jezebel provoke.
God said: "Give Elisha your cloak,
For he is the next one I'll send when
you're gone in a gust of wind."

Elijah appeared once again in accordance with God's plan.
Years later this came to pass in the flesh of John the Baptist.
Who provoked leaders in the land by pointing
to yet another man
This was Jesus, God's only Son, the Messiah,
yes, The promised one.

LESSONS FROM ELIJAH

Elijah was a prophet of God in Gilead. He was not sent to comfort, but rather to confront others with their sin and the consequences to be reaped. Obviously, he was not the most popular man in town, but he knew God. One of the mistakes of Elijah is very familiar to most of us today. He knew God, but wasn't all that sure about others. This made life lonely for Elijah. Others also believed in God and were faithful. They could have been a source of strength and encouragement for Elijah and he for them, but Elijah chose to isolate himself. This isolation could have been a factor in his fear of Jezebel. We can gain courage from others faith. But, on the other hand, Elijah may not have heard the still small voice of God had he been distracted by others. We need to remember we are never truly alone when we belong to God.

Elijah was the most famous and dramatic of Israel's prophets, probably more for his confrontation with the priests of Baal and Asherah than any other recorded events other than his transfiguration with Moses and Jesus. Among his accomplishments we find the prediction of the beginning and the end of a three-year drought and his restoration of the dead child to the Widow of Zarapheh.

One lesson we can learn is that we are never closer to defeat than in our moments of greatest victory. No sooner had Elijah seen the victory on Mount Carmel than we see him heading for the hills, sitting down under a broom tree and praying for death. Then when God appeared to him Elijah had a pity party. We need to learn that even if we don't know who they are, others are faithfully obeying God and fulfilling their duties. We need to realize that God most often reveals himself in a whisper to a heart filled with humility rather than pride. Too often we look for God to reveal himself in the big miracles and miss His guidance. It always comes when we are least expecting it.

EZRA AND NEHEMIAH

In the line of Judah came
A prophet, Ezra was his name.
He spoke out for eighty years;
Persian Kings perked their ears.

Artaxerxes gave him clout,
Permission to rebuild the House.
He wrote books to aid us all
Then helped dedicate the wall.

One who stood by his side,
A common man called Nehemiah.
The office that he held
Was to bear the cup so well.

'Til one day Nehemiah ask
To help the people with their task
Governor of Jerusalem he became,
Relieving oppression his game.

Together they did great things
As though lifted on angel's wings.
In fifty two days they built the wall
Showing God's power to all.

But the best of these two men
Was bringing folks close again
To listen and to heed,
For God would meet their every need.

LESSONS FROM EZRA AND NEHEMIAH

Ezra was first a scribe among the exiles in Babylon. He became the king's envoy and teacher. Eighty years after the rebuilding of the temple under Zerubbabel, Ezra returned to Judah with about 2,000 men and their families.

His task was to begin a program of religious education. His and Nehemiah's authority came from Artaxerxes and gave them significant power.

Ezra is a perfect example of one who was faithful over and few things and God made him a steward over many. Ezra was one of those that God uses as an example of what God can do through ones' life. He was too busy obeying God to keep track of his own successes. His task was to be the one that set the stage for the work that God had for Nehemiah to accomplish.

The two were used by God to start a spiritual movement that swept the nation following the rebuilding of the Jerusalem. One lesson we can learn from his life is the importance of Bible study. A person's willingness to know and practice God's Word will have a direct effect on how God uses them.

Nehemiah was a man of character, persistence and prayer. He was a brilliant planner, had the gift of organization and motivation.

Under his leadership the wall around Jerusalem was rebuilt in 52 days.

We can learn from him to always pray first. We can learn the importance of talking the talk and walking the walk.

Nehemiah was also not afraid to speak the truth in love concerning what God had told him to do.

Because of his faith he could remain calm regardless of the circumstances surrounding him.

Both Ezra and Nehemiah have a lot to teach those who are seeking to be Candidates for the Godly Man of the Year Award.

JOB

Once there was a wealthy man
Who owned vast stock and land.
He had a wife and ten children
There to love and comfort him.

Job feared God and shunned evil.
So Satan moved in for the kill.
He went before God and ask,
To put Job's faith to the task.

God granted Satan's request,
Allowed him to try his test.
First he took Job's stock away,
Death took his children that day.

Still Job praised God's name,
He refused to utter blame.
So Satan ask once again
To inflict personal pain.

With boils from head to foot
Angry words Job took,
"You're better off dead!"
Or so Job's wife said.

Next his three friends came
To try and sort out the blame.
They wanted Job to wail and cry,
Curse God and then ask why.

But Job passed all the test;
He let his faith upon God rest.
Then God gave back to him
Twice what he had back then.

He saw his children four times o'er,
Things were better than before.
He died old and full of years,
Faith strong in spite of tears.

LESSONS FROM JOB

"In the land of Uz there lived a man whose name was Job. This man was blameless and upright; he feared God and shunned evil." So Job and all of his friends thought he had it made! But it was Job's very Godliness that caused Satan to challenge God. You see God called Satan's attention to Job by saying to him, "Have you considered my servant Job? There is no one on earth like him; he is blameless and upright, a man who fears God and shuns evil." Satan counters with "Sure, because you have built a hedge around him, but stretch out your hand and strike everything he has and he will surely curse you to your face." God give Satan permission to do anything he wanted with everything that Job had…the one restriction was "on the man himself do not lay a finger." After Satan had done his worst and still Job did not sin by charging God with wrongdoing Satan and God repeat their initial conversation. Satan now challenges God to test Job by allowing him to bring harm to Job himself. God agrees with the one stipulation to spare Job's life. Satan covered Job with sores from the soles of his feet to the top of his head.

Job's wife withdrew her support and still in all this, Job did not sin in what he said. Then along came Job's "friends". From every corner all humans were asking why and looking for something for Job to confess and repent. It is the same today. Man seems to buy into the law of fairness or justice that is higher and more absolute than God. Even God must act in response to this law in order to be fair. This is the wrong view. The correct view is that God Himself is the standard of justice. He uses his power according to His own moral perfection. Thus, whatever He does is fair, even if we don't understand it. Our response is to appeal directly to Him. Eventually, Job allowed his desire to understand why to overwhelm him and make him question God. To Job's credit he was willing to repent and confess known wrongs, but he was also willing to trust God in spite of unanswered questions. Job learned that knowing God is better than knowing answers. He learned that God is not arbitrary or uncaring and that pain is not always punishment.

God eventually restored and blessed Job's life. He chastised Job's friends then told them that He would have His servant Job to pray for them and that He would accept Job's prayer and not deal with them according to their folly. Then God blessed the latter part of Job's life more than the first. Job lived a hundred and forty years; he saw his children and their children to the fourth generation. And so he died, old and full of years.

This Godly Man suffered much to learn the lessons that can be easily learned from his experience if the Candidates for the Godly Man of the Year will only take heed. The proper response to hard times and questions is confess known sin, call on God for strength, resist self-pity, ask God to open up doors of opportunity and help you discover others who suffer as you do; then accept help from other believers and trust God to work His purpose through you. Recognize that in a sinful world, both good and evil people will suffer, but the good person has God's promise that their suffering will one day come to an end. Don't withdraw inward and give in to the pain, proclaim your faith in God trusting that He cares and will give you the patience to wait upon the Lord.

ISAIAH

Isaiah was a scribe.
A job he thought right
Until upon one day,
He heard the Lord say;

"Isaiah! A prophet you must be
Planted firm like a tree!
Giving out God's words;
But, You won't be heard.

Never mind just carry on
They will hear later on.
Confront them with their sin
Then go and comfort them."

Isaiah never feigned
While five Kings reigned.
The promises that he gave
Were all fulfilled one day.

When God sent His only Son
To redeem us all everyone.
Like Isaiah we should be
Saying "Here am I, send me!"

The reason for his success—
He trusted God knew best.
Forgetting who we are
Releases God's Almighty power.

LESSONS FROM ISAIAH

From Isaiah we can learn that trees and prophets share several characteristics. First, both are planted for the future. Second, both are meant to provide comfort. Both of these characteristics can be difficult. Isaiah discovered that it was hard to provide comfort and stay put in a place where his message was ignored and overlooked. Now God had told him this would be the case, in fact, God compared the people Isaiah served to a tree that would have to be cut down so that a new tree could grow from the old stump. One can understand with this kind of a message why others chose to ignore the message. We can also learn that to effectively confront sin while offering comfort can only be done with God's help. Isaiah took God's pure, perfectly holy, just and loving message to the people by remaining strong and courageous in difficult times.

Isaiah is often referred to as the Prophet of Redemption. His message could be categorized by five "R's". Return, Repent, Renewal, Redemption and Rejoicing! He was used by God as a terrible instrument of Divine Judgments and Messianic Hope. He spoke of the greatness and majesty of God, he emphasized God's holiness and hatred of sin. He focused on the folly of idolatry, God's grace, mercy, love and the blessed rewards of obedience.

Isaiah is remembered as one of the greatest of the Old Testament prophets. He is quoted at least fifty times in the New Testament. Jesus Himself began His public ministry by quoting from Isaiah and applying Isaiah 61 to Himself. His favorite words include, Redeemer, Savior, Counselor, Mighty God, Prince of Peace, Wonderful, and

Everlasting Father. This helps us to know that Isaiah had a relationship with the God of the Universe. He truly knew personally about the very nature of God. It seems this would be a vital part of being a Godly man. Isaiah was also a man that God trusted with information concerning Jesus Christ. Isaiah shared this information so that people would recognize the Messiah as Jesus Christ because he fulfilled all of the prophecies concerning the awaited Messiah. Isaiah told of the Messiah's advent, His virgin birth, of Galilee being the place of His ministry, His deity and the eternity of His throne, His sufferings, His death, His burial, His might, the gentleness of His reign, the righteousness of His reign, His justice, kindness and rule over the Gentiles and about the New Heaven and the New Earth.

Isaiah was like a mighty Oak tree, his most famous quote is "Here am I, Lord, Send me." He knew how to bloom where God planted him and vowed, "I shall not be moved." This man truly could be considered a candidate for the Godly Man of the Year Award. Why even his wife was a prophetess! Take a page out of his book and you will be ahead in the game of Godliness.

JEREMIAH

He persisted, endured and sighed,
The weeping prophet Jeremiah.
As he watched the people trod,
Time and again after other gods.

He spoke, but they would not hear.
He was ignored year after year.
Yet, he felt from up above,
God's very special kind of love.

There was one brief time,
When Judah fell into line,
Eyes were opened and awake;
Crooked lives became straight.

But too soon, Judah yearned,
To their idols they returned.
Jeremiah cried, "Please wait!"
Their response was hate.

'Tho he himself was beaten down
Pain for others was all around.
He knew his heart would be broke
As Judah felt oppression's yoke.

He was there upon the day
Judah was carried away.
To Babylon they did go
Because to God they said, "NO!"

The lesson we can learn,
Is always for God to yearn.
Be faithful no matter what,
With a price your life was bought.

LESSONS FROM JEREMIAH

Jeremiah is known as the "weeping prophet". Perhaps if we had his insight in future events we would weep also. His devotion to God and His efforts to save Jerusalem came at a great sacrifice. It seems sacrifice is one of the chief characteristics of a Godly Man. One of his sacrifices was that he was not permitted to marry as a sign that normal life would soon cease for Jerusalem. Other characteristics of Godliness evident in Jeremiah are endurance, commitment and a caring heart. He was a prophet for forty years, which speaks to these characteristics.

Jeremiah was one of the greatest Hebrew prophets. He was born into the priestly family of Anathoth two and a half miles north east of Jerusalem. His father was Hilkieh. He, with King Josiah, got to be a part of the last religious awakening before the fall to Babylon. His message was one of judgment with an emphasis on inner spiritual character, which is another characteristic of Godliness.

Jeremiah advised submission to Babylon, was accused of treason, thrown into prison, cast into a slimy cistern, given choice by captives to stay in Judah or to go. He chose to stay, but after civil unrest he fled to Egypt.

His life shows us that the majority opinion is not necessarily God's will. We can learn from him that although punishment is severe there is hope in God's mercy. His life also teaches us that serving God does not insure earthly security. In fact, we probably would have considered Jeremiah unfit for a candidate for the Godly Man of the Year Award. Man does not always see what God sees. Jeremiah knew that God knows us intimately and that God's grace sustains!

We can also learn from Jeremiah, the weeping willow tree, that being Godly is never easy, in fact, it can be down right hard. It won't make you popular with man or give you a life of ease on this earth, but…it is worth it all to be in the center of God's will.

DANIEL

To be a prophet one must know
How to pray while here below.
Daniel learned while still young,
It served him well as time went on.

Taken captive as a child,
He refused to be defiled.
Daniel lived each and every day
In a quiet and gentle way.

As a servant to the Kings
He served the food offerings.
But he would not partake
Of what adorned their plate.

continued

The food which Daniel ate
Helped to keep his body great.
The food he fed his soul
Kept him clean and whole.

When Daniel explained a dream
He found favor with a king.
He was to remain a part
Of the King's Royal Court.

King Nebuchadnezzar, on a whim,
Ordered a golden image of him
To be set upon the plain,
His own self to proclaim.

At the sound of flute or lyre,
One was to bow or meet the fire.
But there were three young men
Who would not yield unto this sin.

This increased the King's ire
So he heated up the fire.
When he looked into the door,
He saw not three, but four.

Daniel's three friends below,
Shadrack, Meshack and Abednego.
Had God as their main desire,
He kept them safe from the fire.

"Bring them out and let me see,
There are no burns upon their feet."
Then the king had this to say,
"No other god saves this way."

Daniel once again was ask
If a dream he might grasp.
A tree and writing on the wall,
He foretold the King's fall.

When Darius was then enthroned,
He made a decree of his own.
No one for thirty days,
But to him was to pray.

Daniel who had no guile,
Remained God's obedient child.
Three times each and every day,
He knelt unto God to pray.

Then some very wicked men
Told the king of him.
So'twas ordered then,
Daniel, to the Lion's den.

God shut the mouths of lions,
And after a passage of time
Daniel was free to live again
As a witness to God before men.

Daniel had visions and dreams;
He told of future things.
Then he was told to rest
'Till he was eternally blest.

In exile Daniel spent his days
Yet no ruckus did he raze...
For he knew His God so true
Always takes good care of you.

LESSONS FROM DANIEL

Daniel was born into a Judean family of nobility at the time of King Josiah's reformation. He was taken into captivity by Nebuchadnezzar and trained for three years in the wisdom of the Babylonian Empire. God gave him wisdom, visions and interpretations. Daniel was wise and took advantage of opportunity without letting opportunity take advantage of him. He stood by his convictions no matter what. Daniel held strongly to the faith he had learned as a child. A lesson to be learned here is the importance of training up our children in the way they should go so that when they are old they will not depart from it. Daniel lived his entire life in a place he did not want to be. What makes him a good candidate for the Godly Man of the Year Award is his faith that kept him steady in the boat of life's circumstance and beyond. Daniel always did what was right in the eyes of the Lord even at the possibility of death. He also was an exemplary witness for God to pagan people not only in his steadfastness, but in the way he served and treated them. Now that does seem to be a lesson for today. Too often, we are easily swayed because of circumstances and revengeful spirits.

Daniel learned that God can and does use people wherever they are especially if they keep themselves from any impurity, if they stand with courage against compromise, and trust Him for deliverance and victory. We often see Daniel in the Lion's Den as a young man. The truth is he was past eighty and still doing the Godly thing. Too often today we hear the phrase, "been there, done that, bought the tee shirt". To be Godly means we never retire, we stay strong until God calls us home. Daniel saw God's victories in his life for over 90 years and then was taken home to his reward. Don't you wonder if he ever looks down and says "I told you so!" It's easy to have Daniel's faith if you remember when you are a part of God's family...in the end, you win.

Another of Daniel's strengths was his love of scripture. He stayed in God's word for information, instruction and comfort. He never felt he knew it all...he always knew there was more for him in God's Word. Daniel was never disappointed...surprised, yes, but never disappointed. How much time do you spend in God's Word? Now lest we think it was easy for Daniel, after all, he was a part of the Kings Court, let's look back at his prayers. Even though Daniel probably lived an opulent life style, he longed to go home. That is why he prayed facing Jerusalem. His heart was waiting for the spirit of the Lord to return to the Temple in Jerusalem. He prayed for God's mercy on the Hebrew people. He never forgot who he was or where he came from. In his longest prayer, Daniel identified with the people's sins at least 32 times realizing that all have sinned. Daniel did not believe his press...his press said that no fault could be found in Daniel. Daniel was heart-broken and longed for God's mercy. He was consistent and persistent in his prayer life. Because prayer had been a way of life for him, he was prepared when life was hard. We can learn from him to not wait until we are in a tough situation to learn to pray. We can learn to always do the Godly thing wherever you are and let God take care of the lions. There will always be lions, furnaces, captivity and evil until Jesus comes again. Learn to trust in God's mercy, judgment and protection. Then you, like Daniel, can be a good candidate for the Godly Man of the Year Award.

HOSEA (Salvation)

The prophet called Hosea heard the Lord one day;
"Go today and take a bride,
one who'll stray from your side."
It seemed a strange request, but God knows what is best.
Hosea was soon to discover, Gomer was loved by another.

The children that she bore foretold what was in store.
God's message was in their names;
There was a price for playing games
Gomer reached her rope's end because of all her sin.
Hosea bought her for a price; brought her back into his life.

Hosea's life was his prophecy, it told of things to be.
Israel was God's bride, ever straying from his side.
God's love is faithful and true—
there is nothing He won't do.
He tempered judgment with His grace,
to those who loved raisin cakes.

Only one thing does He seek, before He offers up relief.
'Tis a sincere confessing that will bring His blessing.
Someday the bridegroom will come
to take His bride back home.
He has redeemed your life. He paid the ultimate price.

HOSEA

Hosea was a prophet of God in 759-725 B. C. He had the task of presiding over his beloved nation as it gasps its dying breath. Hosea is identified in the book bearing his name as a genuine prophet to whom "the word of the Lord" came. This tells us the source of his authority and describes his credentials. It also teaches us the importance of authenticity. His messages focused on judgment while holding out hope of national revival based on radical repentance. Hope was his mantra. Not only did Hosea have a message, he was asked to live out that message. It's one thing to speak a word from God and quite another to allow your life to be the message from God. It looks like we just might have a Candidate for the Godly Man of the Year Award in this prophet named Hosea.

First, let's take a look at his name. Hosea's personal name means salvation. In his day your name indicated what you would become…Hosea's parents named him well. His message was one of hope for salvation. Second, let's look at his personal life. God told him to take a wife of harlotry and to have children of harlotry "for the land hath committed great whoredom, departing from the Lord." In other words, God told him to take a wife who would be unfaithful to him and who would bear children fathered by other men. Then it was predicted that his wife, Gomer, would leave him to pursue her lusts. Hosea was instructed to find her, redeem her and bring her home again, fully reconciled. God was asking Hosea to experience on a personal level what God was experiencing with the nation of Israel and still experiences with us today. All of his experiences were images of God's love, judgment, grace and mercy. This experience was to help Hosea see what being Godly entailed. God is pictured as husband, father, lion, leopard, bear, dew, rain, moth and other things. Israel is pictured as wife, sick person, vine, grapes, early fruit, olive tree, woman in childbirth, oven, morning mist, chaff and smoke to name a few.

Hosea dramatically portrays God's constant and persistent love. He submitted himself willingly to God's direction; he grieved with Him over the unfaithfulness of his wife and His people; he heard the clear warnings of judgment and the need for repentance. We can certainly learn from Hosea that faithfulness to God requires obedience, sacrifice, and unconditional love, a forgiving spirit, and a persistent heart. We can also learn of the faithfulness required to vows that are made. Perhaps one lesson sometimes overlooked is that if we desire to be Godly, we need to remember that we are to be the "instrument to Salvation" to all those around us. We are to search out the lost, take them into the presence of God where Christ comes and makes His home in their hearts, forgiving, redeeming, justifying and reconciling all who have gone astray

JOEL (Jehovah is God-author of book)

"The day of the Lord will come!"
These words spoke Pethuel's son.
It was to Judah that Joel spoke concerning
laws they had broke.
For life was good it seemed as
they planned and they schemed.
But as God looked down, Joel saw He wore a frown.

For God settles all accounts, beware,
if you His name renounce.
The crooked will be made straight
e're we enter heaven's gate.
Joel warned of a "locust plague" to make their spirits lag.
Said; "t'would be but the start,
if they changed not their heart"

Israel, in the north, counted not man's worth
So God sent a shepherd man to face them with their sin
Punishment and forgiveness were often stressed
But when death beckons it is with God man must reckon!

AMOS (Burden Bearer)

Amos spoke in metaphors, using common laymen's chores.
He was not at all afraid, as he the Lord obeyed.
But the last words he spoke were ones of glorious hope
God would make them great again,
if they would follow God's plan

OBADIAH (Servant of Jehovah)

Obadiah was sent into Edom who had from Esau come.
And though blood related, the Israelites they hated.
When Israel had a curse, Edom helped to make it worse.
They laughed and they hooted as their
brother's house was looted.

So in poetic verse, Obadiah told the worst.
"As you have done unto the Jew, it will be returned to you."
Obadiah wasn't playing a game, nor was he placing blame.
He sounded the alarm...Don't bring God's people harm.

Three prophets who spoke for God
the little while they trod,
Not much else of them we know
about their lives here below.

LESSON FROM JOEL, AMOS AND OBADIAH

Joel was a prophet who spoke forthrightly and force-fully. Very little is known about him personally. His message was one of foreboding and warning but also filled with hope. He prophesied to the Southern Kingdom, Judah. He had a vision of the power and might of God and of God's ultimate judgment of sin. He urged his people to see that God had allowed rebellion, but soon "the Day of the Lord" would come. This is in fact the theme of his book, He affirmed that God shows kindness and gives blessing to all who call on the name of the Lord. Joel prophecies of judgment were meant to motivate others to choose to follow, obey and worship God who alone is the Sovereign God. We can learn from Joel that Godliness requires having a vision of God while at the same time seeing the fallacies of men. A Godly man uses his energies and insight to lead others into the paths of righteousness. He reminds us to teach our history to our children so that they can learn from it. But he also teaches us the blessings of worship.

~~~~~~~~~~~~~~~~~~~~~

Amos, on the other hand, was a burden bearer. In fact, his personal name means "a load". His people were a heavy load he carried. Amos was also not a proclaimed prophet or from a priestly family. He was what we would call a "layperson". In other words, his only credentials were "God told me". He was called by God to speak God's words to Israel, The Northern Kingdom. He was as one lonely voice prophesying from both the desert and the villages. Amos was a simple man with a significant message. He was used to spending his days herding sheep and tending sycamore-fig trees. He could have stayed home, took care of his family feeling secure in his personal relationship with God, but God gave him a vision and he obeyed God which proves Amos was, not only a man of God, but a great Candidate for the Godly Man of the Year Award. We learn from Amos to be all God wants us to be regardless of recognition from man.

The people of the Northern Kingdom were enjoying a time of peace and prosperity and had grown quite complacent in their relationship with God and others. In fact, as is ever the case, the better their life became the more they judged and oppressed others. Amos' most famous message was "But, let justice roll on like a river, righteousness like a never-failing stream." Amos' message was timely for his day, but also for today. Godly men don't become complacent, allowing things and events to take God's place in their lives. They are busy helping the poor and oppressed, bearing one another's burdens. God is still calling men today. A Godly man hears the call, sees the vision and answers the call. He takes a stand and covers the ground on which he stands.

~~~~~~~~~~~~~~~~~~~~~~~~~

Obadiah, whose name means "servant of the Lord' is also a prophet of which little is known except his effectiveness in being obedient to God. Obadiah's message can be summed up in his words, "The day of the Lord is near for all nations. As you have done, it will be done to you; your deeds will return upon your own head." Perhaps being a Godly man is being a man of a few well-chosen words.

JONAH

If you would see God's mercy and His grace,
Just put yourself in Jonah's place.
He learned the gospel is for all;
Belief and repentance death forestall.

The city of Nineveh did not deserve,
God's grace was Jonah's word.
But he knew God would forgive
If they changed the way they lived.

So when God sent him to their land,
Jonah made up another plan.
He in a ship did set sail;
Wound up in a giant whale.

Three days within it's belly
Turned his knees into jelly.
When he was spit upon the sand,
He obeyed God's command.

Nineveh heard and did repent,
But Jonah pitched a fit.
He complained and did deride.
God rebuked him for his pride.

Years later, when Jesus came
He mentioned Jonah's name.
The story of this prophet's strife
Portrayed Jesus death and eternal life.

And we like Nineveh of old,
Who deserve worse than to be scold
Can receive the compassion and the love
Of our blessed Savior up above.

LESSONS FROM JONAH

There is a country-western song titled, "An Attitude Adjustment". Now that is exactly what the prophet, Jonah, needed. You see, God loves all people and He expects his Godly men to love all people, but some men today, like Jonah, have folks they don't quite "cotton to". These folks for Jonah were the people of Nineveh, a city and a king who were known enemies to God. God tells Jonah to go and preach to Nineveh and Jonah says basically, "have you lost your mind?" Jonah wanted God to destroy the city, it's people and their king. God wanted to offer them mercy and grace. So Jonah decided to run. A lesson here is you cannot run from God. He is ahead of you, behind you, beside you, over you and under you. His eyes are on you all the time, not to catch you doing something wrong, but rather to guide and protect you.

Under circumstances only God can bring to pass, Jonah found himself in the water, in the whale, on his knees and beached, so he reluctantly agreed to go to Nineveh. He preached, the people repented and turned to God then Jonah pitched a fit. He was a "Pharisee' before his time. This act of God was a rebuke to Jonah and Israel because they thought themselves better than others...even though they refused to respond to God's message. God forgives all who turn from their sin and accept His Grace. God's message of love and forgiveness was and is not for one, It is for all.

The people of Nineveh, the Assyrians, didn't deserve God's mercy, but they repented and God spared them. Likewise, Jonah was not rejected for aborting his mission and having a bad attitude. God has great love, patience and forgiveness. He offers this love indiscriminately to those who are in the bondage of sin and to those who have strayed from the fold.

Our lesson from Jonah is first of all to remember, when you end up in the water, the whale and beached, you need to get down on your knees. Second, we don't have to understand God's direction we just have to follow His instruction. Third, because of God's great mercy and love no one has to get what they deserve. Fourth, God is the God of the second, third, "to affinity and beyond" chance. He expects us to follow His example and learn the lesson of patience and forgiveness. Fifth, to be a Candidate for The Godly Man of the Year Award one has to see others as God sees them and offer them the same grace God has given to all who turn to Him. "For God so loved the world, He gave"! He expects, no demands, the same of all who aspire to Godliness.

MICAH (Who is like God?)

Fifty-five years Micah warned
Trouble comes when God is scorned.
Repent for pardon of your sin,
Stop oppressing other men.

His message had three parts,
All said, "Listen with your heart."
Each closed with a promise
For all those God called His.

Micah spoke to both kingdoms,
Reminding of all God had done.
"Walk Humbly" was the word
To receive mercy from the Lord.

NAHUM (Compassionate)

Another spoke of woes to come
He was called Nahum.
A word of comfort he gave;
Nineveh would not be saved.

God was angry once again,
His plan was made plain.
Nineveh would surely fall,
While Judah again stood tall.

LESSONS FROM MICAH AND NAHUM

Micah was a prophet to the Northern Kingdom, Israel, and the Southern Kingdom, Judah during the reigns of Jotham, Ahaz and Hezekiah. There were false prophets, dishonest leaders and selfish priests who carried out religious ceremonies for the wrong reasons. They were self-seeking individuals who were after money and influence. This mixing of selfish motives and empty display of religion adds up to a perverted faith. Oppression ran rampant. Micah emphasized the need for justice and peace. He promised he birth of the Messiah hundreds of years before Christ's birth. He even told the place of His birth and that His plan was to restore His people. He preached that God's greatest desire is not empty sacrifice and worship. God delights in faith that produces justice, love for others and obedience to Him. Micah's words, "He has showed you, O man, what is good, And what does the Lord require of you? To act justly and to love mercy and to walk humbly with your God." These words offer the answer to the question, "What is required to become a Godly Man?"

~~~~~~~~~~~~~~~~~~~~~~~~~~~~~

Nahum, like Jonah, was a prophet to Nineveh, the capital of the Assyrian Empire and he prophesied between 663-612 B. C. While Jonah had seen Nineveh repent and receive God's grace over a hundred years before, things had changed. The city had fallen back into wickedness. Now is this a familiar theme? Assyria was a world power that seemed unstoppable as they forged their power across the continent. They were cruel and ruthless to the conquered people. It became Nahum's task to proclaim God's anger against Assyria's evil. His message was also a warning to Judah because they were falling into the trap of wanting to be like the Assyrians. Over and over, history proves that Satan welds a mighty stick with people wanting to be like other people instead of striving toward Godliness. Mankind seems to buy into the idea that seeming worldly success is a blessing from God. Judah bought into the idea that the Assyrians seemed to have all the power and passions they wanted so i.e. to get that power and those possessions, they must become like the Assyrians. We forget that God allows evil to prosper at times to achieve His purposes. His message through Nahum is those who do evil and oppress others will one day meet a bitter end. All that glitters is not gold. The Assyrians fell to the Babylonians, who fell to the Medes and Persians who fell to the Greeks who fell to the Romans and so on it goes. One day all will fall before Almighty God. Modern man would like to think he has evolved to a more enlightened awareness, but hey, what about the Joneses, the grass is greener mentality. A Godly man learns to pay attention to history...to remember The Lord our God is a jealous God. We need to always be aware that history is really "His story".

HABAKKUK (Embrace)

There once was a prophet and Habakkuk was his name,
He went before the Lord for to whine and complain.
For the nation that he served had cause for shame,
They sought for the Lord to saddle with the blame.

Now the tribe of Judah had an awful smell,
For rampant sin had 'em doomed to hell.
Ole Habakkuk was a feelin' mighty stressed,
By all of this sin and the wickedness.

The days were dark and defeat was near.
God's judgment seemed quite drear.
What Habakkuk found so hard to comprehend,
Was that God would use even more wicked men.

Perplexed and confused, Habakkuk climbed the tower,
To seek the Lord, ask help for the hour.
God was not watching nor did He care,
But the prophet found God was there.

"How long shall I cry and God not hear!"
Ole Habakkuk shouted out, loud and clear.
But God's reply left little doubt,
Why, it made the ole prophet want to shout.

For Habakkuk had waited quite expectantly,
Hoping God's plan was to set them free.
But what he heard was a great surprise,
God pronounced woes of which there were five.

God allows testing to burn out the dross,
For every evil He extracts a cost.
He may take ages just to show His plan,
But in the end, the just will stand.

When the faithful go to God a lookin' for a choice,
He always gives 'em reasons to rejoice.
Ole Habakkuk sang out into the night,
The beauty of his song showed his delight.

God works out His purpose and in His time,
The choice to trust, now that's yours and mine.
We may never see the smallest part.
We just need to trust His heart.

We should trust that God knows best,
He cares and listens to our requests.
He proclaims the just shall live by faith,
Now that's the part that is really great.

All of this happened a way back when,
Not a lot of difference in now and then.
Praise God, now we are under grace,
Just keep a lookin' in God's sweet face.

Now if there are times you don't understand,
Why not try old Habakkuk's plan,
Just get in line and join the band,
That sings and shouts, "Ain't God Grand!"

LESSONS FROM HABAKKUK

Habakkuk was a prophet who had a lot of questions so he sought solutions. He also knew where to go to get the right answers. Habakkuk went to the source, he went to the Lord! Then he waited on the answers. Now that is a novel idea. Then when he received the answers he responded with faith. He believed God! Wow! He didn't just believe in God. He believed God. What a difference there would be if we could learn this lesson from Habakkuk. You see the problem is not with God, it is with our limited understanding of God and His ways

Habakkuk saw a dying world and it broke his heart. He did not have the answers, but he knew the God who did so he took his questions to God. His questions are really rather interesting, in that they are the same questions we still ask today. For instance:

How long must I call for help?

Why is there evil?

Why does evil seem to be winning all the time?

Why do You make me look at injustice?

Why do You tolerate wrong?

Why do You tolerate the treacherous?

Once he had pled his case, Habakkuk stayed put and waited until the answer came.

God's answer was an exhaustive list of the sins and idols of the people!

Now Habakkuk had a new understanding of God's power and love. He knew that God's timing is perfect and that faith supplies the answers. He also heard God's promise for the future for those who are faithful. We can learn from Habakkuk to move from doubt to faith. Then we, like Habakkuk can rejoice in who God is and what He will do. We will know that the just (righteous) shall live by faith. The Apostle Paul learned this from Habakkuk's writings and made it the central element in his theology. Then through Paul this message came alive for Martin Luther setting off the Protestant Reformation. This so-called minor prophet had a major influence on those who followed him. The Godly man of today can have just that major of an influence if he learns from Habakkuk to take his questions to God, wait patiently for the answer, then respond with faith, stand firm and rejoice in the future God has for those who love Him. Then we can say with Habakkuk, "The Sovereign Lord is My Strength; He makes my feet like the feet of the deer, He enables me to go to the heights!" Godly men spend a lot of time on the mountain tops acquiring the strength for the valleys.

ZEPHANIAH (Hidden of the Lord)
HAGGAI
ZECHARIAH (Jehovah Remembers)
MALACHI (Messenger of the Lord)

Four more prophets had God's eye,
Zephaniah, Haggai, Zechariah and Malachi.
Each had a very special place,
In helping God's plan to trace.

Zephaniah tried to stop the apathy,
Told them from pride to flee.
Haggai got a nation on its feet,
God's temple to complete.

Zechariah revealed deliverance,
A Messiah, their only chance.
Malachi attempted to restore
A relationship with God once more.

Malachi tried asking questions;
While Zechariah shared his visions,
Zephaniah spoke of terror and pain,
Haggai's words were direct and plain.

Yet, each of these prophet men
Promised there was hope again
For the future would one day bring
The glorious coming of Zion's King.

LESSONS FROM ZEPHANIAH, HAGGAI, ZECHARIAH AND MALACHI

Zephaniah was also a minor prophet, whatever that means. Personally I don't think God has a minor anything. Actually, the difference in a major and a minor prophet has to do with the length of the books written by them as recorded in scripture. There are four Major Prophets, Isaiah, Jeremiah, Ezekiel and Daniel. The remaining twelve are referred to as Minor Prophets. It is important that we recognize the designation is man-made not made by God. God has a way of choosing those the world thinks of as minor to accomplish the major tasks in order that He alone will be glorified. We do know that Zephaniah was a descendant of Hezekiah but which Hezekiah is debated. He could have been the son of a King or a Cushite. The latter would give him a connection to Judah. The former would have made him a prince who could have done something about the national climate of his day. We'll have to look him up when we get to heaven and ask, but in the meantime, let's just learn from his experience in serving God

Zephaniah became a prophet about the same time as Josiah became the king, around 640 B.C. It is believed he was a major influence on the revival that took place under Josiah's reign. The climate of the times was "Happy Daze"! By that I mean the people were prosperous, seemingly secure and safe, but no longer cared about God. They felt no sorrow for their sins, which were many. God's demands for righteous living were irrelevant to them because their sense of security came from their wealth. The Priests worshipped Baal, Moleck and the starry hosts. They mixed pagan practices with pseudo faith in God. Does this not sound like today's news?

Zephaniah had a word from God that God's punishment was on the way...but that was not bad because it would truly be a "Happy Day!" He had a little trouble selling that idea just as we do today, but never the less that is a truth we all need to share with others. You see it will be a happy day because God has promised to purify the people, to remove the proud from Mt. Zion, to purge away all sins and evil, to restore His people and to give them hope! Zephaniah's message is contained in the song, "Oh Happy Day". It goes something like this: "Oh Happy Day, Oh Happy Day, when Jesus washed my sins away. Oh Happy Day! He taught me how to watch and pray, Oh Happy Day. He taught me how to live rejoicing every day, Oh Happy Day!" This needs to be our theme song as we await that happy day..that day when Jesus comes again. That is the day that Zephaniah was prophesying about. We need to learn to live in that promise as we live each day, not searching for happiness based on happenings, but resting in the assurance that the Happy Day is a sure thing for those that repent of their sins, ask forgiveness and invite Jesus into their hearts.

The last three Old Testament Prophets, Haggai, Zechariah and Malachi prophesied to the Jews after they returned from exile to Jerusalem. Haggai was determined to persuade the people to rebuild the Temple. It was no easy task to move a discouraged nation to rise up and build a Temple, but he did it. Zechariah was the prophet of restoration and glory. Malachi is the bridge between the Old and New Testaments. A silence of 400 years lies between Malachi and John's voice crying in the wilderness. All were Godly Men!

GOSPELS

JOHN THE BAPTIST

Four hundred years, and not a word
from God above had been heard.
Then the people got their wish,
God spoke thru John the Baptist.
From the desert John the Baptist came,
the coming of a Savior to proclaim.
He had known for all of his life, He was to be a Nazarite.

For the angel before his birth,
told his father of his worth
He did not live like other men,
appearances did not concern him.
People were drawn to his words;
too long the truth had not been heard.
He said, "Repent and be baptized",
then he pointed into the skies.

"Look for one to take my place
whose shoes I'm not fit to lace."
Never once did he claim reverence unto his own name.
But one day beside a river, John began to quiver.
"Look the Lamb of God comes on yonder sod!"

He will take away your sin, if you, but turn to him.
Jesus he baptized out of love. The Spirit came as a dove.
Then God spoke thru the trees,
"This is my Son, I am pleased."
John said again out loud, "This is the Son of God!"

John continued to confront; speaking words, oh so blunt.
Until he was put into jail because King Herod he did rail.
The problem was Herod's wife,
because of her, John lost his life.
Salome danced before the king until
he did John's head bring.

But it was all to no avail for John his mission did not fail.
He had announced upon the earth,
the Messiah's royal birth.
The one whose coming had been expected,
would soon be rejected.
But all was not lost, for Jesus,
the awaited Messiah paid the cost.

LESSONS FROM JOHN THE BAPTIST

'Ya lookin for Godly? Tadah! John the Baptist recognized Jesus while they were both still in the womb! They were relatives! Don't you wonder what was in John's heart as he and Jesus spent time together as children? Now scripture nor history gives us any details that they ever saw each other before the baptism of Jesus, but being from Jewish families, they must have been together at least at special occasions, holidays, family reunions and ect. They could have even played together as children. We do know that John's mother was an important contact person for Mary the mother of Jesus. John always knew that he and Jesus had a special role to play in this world. John knew that his role was to announce the coming of the Savior. We know that he stirred in his mother's womb when the expectant Mary approached. We know that he was in the desert when God's words of direction came to him, but John was ready and waiting. The angel who had announced his birth to his father Zechariah had made it clear this child was to be one set apart for God's service, a Nazirite. John never swayed from this calling.

John was not interested in fashion, culinary delights, or the latest political situation. John had a message from God. He never had power or position in the Jewish political system, yet he spoke with such authority that people responded to his message by the hundreds because they knew he spoke the truth. John's theme was repentance and he was uncompromising in his confrontation. He challenged all to repent of their sins and be baptized as a sign of that repentance. In fact, this is where he acquired the name of the baptizer which time has shortened to "the Baptist". Could the thing that made John attract so many followers have been his relationship to Jesus? It certainly was not his appearance, social standing or wealth. It was just who and what he knew.

John's life could not have been an easy one and we know it was not a safe one. He gave his life because he confronted Herod with his sin, but not before he pointed others to Jesus Christ there by the Jordan River as he baptized our Lord. John knew that God had a plan for his life and he invested in that plan because he knew that there is something more valuable than life itself.

Ya wanna be Godly? Accept that God has a plan for each of our lives. His plan is for us to be Godly. John gives us a perfect footprint to follow. You just pursue a personal relationship with Jesus Christ, make Him the focus of your life, have the courage of your convictions and commit your all to sharing the truth you know everywhere you go. God will use you in a way He can use no one else because you are an integral part of His over all plan for the salvation of all mankind.

GOSPELS

JOSEPH AND MARY

Nazareth 'twas the place, Joseph first saw her face.
Mary was such a delight, he would have her for his wife.
Joseph loved this young girl, she was his whole world.
But then on one night, he got an awful fright.

What was that she said? Oh! He wished he were dead.
For Mary was with child, now she was all defiled.
God came to him and said; "Let go of all your dread,
The baby that is to be born, was conceived of the Lord.

The child within her womb will change
the world very soon."
So Joseph took Mary aside, she became his new bride.
They trusted and obeyed, listened to what God said.
Pondering within their hearts, each and every little part.

Then upon His birth, and time while on earth,
They nurtured, loved and gave to
the one who came to save.
A carpenter by trade, Joseph many things made.
He did the best he could with what he understood.

Mary watched as her Son on the cross the victory won.
Thankful within her heart, that God gave her a special part.
Life for them was not easy, often made them feel queasy.
But when your faith is strong, God will right every wrong.

LESSONS FROM JOSEPH

First off, let's just say that Joseph surely had to be a Godly man! God was going to give him the awesome task of being the legal and earthly father of the Son of God! That tells me that God knew this man's heart was Godly. Scripture tells us that he was a righteous man, a man of integrity and one who would recognize the voice of an angel.

But let's not forget that he was also a human man who was concerned about the mores of society. Joseph was also a man in love. No matter what the circumstances of his engagement to Mary we know he loved her by his actions. Love is always putting another ahead of oneself. No human has ever done this better than Joseph.

Joseph was looking forward to his marriage to Mary when she comes to him and tells him that she is expecting God's child. He knows the child is not his, so who could fault him for his concern. But instead of condemning Mary, Joseph tries to find a solution that will spare Mary's life. Notice that God honors Joseph's love for Mary by sending an angel to verify Mary's story. Then God offered another plan, marry Mary and honor her virginity until the baby was born. Joseph followed God's plan all the way to a stable in Bethlehem, through the flight to Egypt to escape Herod, back to Nazareth where he helped Mary raise Jesus. He knew all of the worries of fatherhood as Jesus was "lost" when returning from the Temple in Jerusalem after the Passover, he endured the looks and questions as to Jesus' paternity, he taught Jesus his trade of carpentry. Joseph surely helped Jesus learn to walk, to talk, and gave Him a Godly earthly home.

Joseph is not mentioned after Jesus is twelve years of age. Tradition says that he died. But we do know that he left a legacy of love for his family and a shining example of a Godly man for all. We know that he was a person who was sensitive to God's guidance and willing to follow that guidance regardless of the personal cost. This is a valuable lesson for those who are seeking to be Godly.

One more thing to consider from the life of Joseph is the earthly rewards of being Godly.

Imagine, if you can, the joys of watching the Son of God grow up in your home. The thrill of each new development must have been invigorating as it brought wonder of all that lay ahead. Then there had to be great satisfaction as he looked into the eyes full of love that met him at the break of each new day from his beloved Mary. After all doing the right thing for the right reason is a reward in and of itself.

GOSPELS & ACTS

JAMES AND JOHN

Two brothers, John and James,
Followed Jesus when He came
A walking by the sea,
Saying, "Come follow me."

Sons of Thunder, they were called,
We think of them with awe,
For each of them had a part-
A special place in Jesus heart.

'Tho they did not understand
All that encompassed God's plan;
They stayed close beside the Man
Right up until the end.

And when at last they knew
What they were meant to do,
They were willing to die,
Because they now knew why.

James, the older of the two
Was the first to see the view
Of heaven's pearly gate
Where his Savior did await.

John remained with work to do,
He served the Lord long and true.
He was exiled for a while,
In the sea, upon Patmo's isle.

'Twas there he had a dream
When God shared with him some things
About Jesus, His only Son
And the second time He would come.

LESSONS FROM JOHN

In the accompanying portrait of John, the artist seems to capture an expression that says, "I know a secret!" The Disciple John certainly knew several secrets as we see recorded in his writings. These secrets are lessons in our quest for Godliness. We know from John's relationship to Jesus and others that he is a major candidate for the Godly Man of the Year Award. Let's examine some of John's secrets.

Secret number one is that love changes people. One who is loved is able to love others. John was the recipient of the love of Jesus Christ. He always referred to himself as the disciple Jesus loved. Now we know that Jesus loved all the disciples then and now, but the love of Jesus in one's life makes one feel loved exclusively. That is what the personal relationship is all about. The realization that Jesus came, gave His life, was resurrected, ascended to heaven and is coming again for ME! Greater love hath no man...John was so loved that his life, ministry and writings are focused around that love. He even recorded Jesus saying, "By this (love) all men will know you are my disciples". John understood that to receive this love meant one is to give that same love away to others that they my know Christ. So it follows, a Godly man will love God and others.

Secret number two is God changes lives, not personalities. He takes personalities and uses them to accomplish the purposes of His plan for each life. John and his brother James were referred to by Jesus as the "Sons of Thunder." Now it doesn't take much of an imagination to know why. Let's see, James and John suggested that Jesus give them permission to call down fire from heaven on a village that had not welcomed them and Jesus. Not exactly an example of Godliness. Then there was the occasion where they were arguing over who would be the greatest and the asking for special privilege when Jesus came into His Kingdom. It seems that James and John shared a tendency to outbursts of selfishness and anger. God can and does use even the negative tendencies to give those seeking Godliness perspective in dealing with others.

Secret number three is God decides the course of each life. This secret was revealed to John when Jesus was explaining to Peter what was ahead for Peter. Peter asked, what about John? Jesus replied, "That is not your concern." In today's vernacular that would read, "That's for me to know and you to find out." A part of Godliness is getting one's own life in order before attempting to meddle in the lives of others.

Secret number four is God is never out of control. John reveals learning this truth in the sharing of his revelation of things to come. While things may appear out of control, a Godly man knows that nothing happens without God's knowledge and or permission. Godliness is working within God's plan, not attempting to direct God.

Secret number five is when we accept God's gift of grace, in the end, we win! Now this secret should put a twinkle in the eye of every candidate for The Godly Man of the Year Award!

GOSPELS & ACTS

ANDREW AND PETER

Two brothers in the sand, casting nets with their hand,
Heard the man from Galilee as He walked beside the sea.
"Come along with me and be Fishers of Men', said He.
They dropped their nets that very day,
followed Jesus without delay.

Andrew helped to feed the mob as he marveled at the job.
While upon Mount Olivet he asked
the Lord what He meant.
When of the temple Jesus spoke,
being destroyed and all broke,
Then being built up again. These words puzzled him.

Simon Peter on the other hand,
became the leader of the band.
For his potential Jesus sought when
He renamed him the Rock.
Peter often spoke before he thought,
this great sadness to Jesus brought.
But Jesus knew within his heart were
seeds enough for a start.

'Tis true he denied one day the one
he had promised to obey.
He did it three times as Jesus had said when they dined.
He was then truly blest when he along with the rest
Knew Jesus Christ was alive; death's blow He had denied.

Peter was glad once again to go upon the mountain.
There he heard Jesus ask, "Peter, are you up to the task?"
But Jesus already knew Peter would know what to do.
The zeal of this one man helped share God's eternal plan.

Peter was one of three who were blest to be,
The very closest ones to God's only Begotten Son.
This man who walked upon the sea,
became all he was meant to be.
He kept his eyes upon the Lord,
taught and lived by His word.

He saw visions, healed the sick,
even foiled a magician's trick.
Angels brought his release from prisons unto peace.
Tradition says he died one day,
but not in a regular sort of way.
On his cross his head was down as he
to heaven was bound.

LESSONS FROM PETER

Simon, whom Jesus renamed Peter, was a fisherman turned disciple. Both of these facts teach us the primary lesson we can learn from this Godly man. Godly men are not perfect, nor do they have to be. Man is not born Godly. He must evolve into Godliness as he is changed by the love and the touch of the Master. God most often, chooses the weak so the world can see His strength and glorify Him. A Godly man is always a vehicle through which others can see Christ. God's faithfulness can compensate for our greatest unfaithfulness.

But, don't you just love Peter? Good ole foot-in mouth Peter. You can't fault his enthusiasm. He lived under the motto, "Nothing ventured, nothing gained." Jesus saw in this man the potential to be the voice of the Gospel after Pentecost. History proves that once again, God knows what He is doing in all circumstances. Why is that such a hard concept for man? It just could be because of the forces of evil that convince man that he should be in control. While Peter often spoke and acted without thinking, he learned to obey God's direction and became all God intended for him to be. He was the recognized leader of Jesus' disciples. He was a part of the inner circle of three who were closest to Jesus. His motives, for the most part, were good intentioned. We can learn from Peter, that lessons learned from mistakes made are the life lessons we take to heart and live by.

It is through Peter's greatest mistake, the denying of Jesus, that we gain insight into the awesome mercy and forgiveness of our Savior. We would do well to ask ourselves on a regular basis the question Jesus asked Peter. "Do you love me more than these?" These, what? Other disciples? The world? Perhaps there is a vagueness in this question to cover anything that would come before God. Jesus saw in Peter potential. He saw in Peter the potential to be changed by His love, the vigor to take that love to others, the example of acceptance by God offered to all, even those who fail.

God was not disappointed by Peter. His faith grew as steadfast as a Rock. Peter overcame his prejudice and took the Gospel to the Gentiles and beyond. Peter gave his life for the cause of Christ in one final act of humility. He asked to be crucified upside down because he did not feel worthy to die in the same manner as his Lord. He is still teaching us how to be Godly in spite of our short comings. We learn from Peter that God works through flawed vessels that are moldable in His hands. Jesus took this fisherman and made Him the greatest Fisher of Men the world has ever known. He wants to do the same with you. Jesus is calling all to be Candidates for the Godly Man of the Year Award saying, "Come follow me and I will MAKE you..."

GOSPELS

SEVEN DISCIPLES

Jesus chose some common men,
But He had special jobs for them.
Matthew left his lucrative post
For the One he loved the most.

Jesus had a purpose for his pen,
To record all that was to transcend.
He called Phillip and Bartholomew,
They had some preaching to do.

Thomas was the doubting one,
Until he touched the risen Son.
There was Thaddeus and James,
Both martyrs, they became.

Then there was Simon the Zealot,
A very different and unlikely sort.
They came from all walks,
To hear the Master talk.

Day by day they walked with Him,
Lived as though they were His kin.
Yet, when Jesus most needed them,
Suddenly the crowd grew thin.

For they did not understand
Even tho He shared His plan.
But as they saw all was not lost,
Each was willing to pay the cost.

To have seen the Risen Lord,
Made it easy, not hard.
It's the same for you and me,
If we would disciples be.

LESSONS FROM SEVEN DISCIPES

Jesus chose twelve disciples. He called out and said, "Follow Me." Eleven of the disciples followed Jesus to death. One was truly never a "follower". To be a "follower" means to 'lose it all to gain everything' according to the lyrics of a gospel song recorded by Jesse Dixon. Judas, John, James, Peter and Andrew are examined elsewhere. The seven disciples we learn from here are: Philip, Bartholomew, Thomas, Matthew, James the son of Alphaeus, Thaddaeus and Simon the Zealot.

We learn from Philip that we are to feed the hungry, literally and spiritually. We are to be traveling missionaries taking the gospel to all people. We are to learn so that we might explain with better understanding. Philips' life presents us with a challenge. To those outside of Christ, he is a reminder that the gospel is for you. To those who have accepted Christ, he is a reminder that we are not to disqualify anyone from God's grace. We are to give others the same grace given to us. Philip's faithfulness and zeal for sharing the gospel is as important today as it was in inspiring the Ethiopian Eunuch and the Apostle Paul to go and do likewise.

We learn from Thomas the importance of knowing the truth. Thomas gets a bad rap for being a "Doubting Thomas", but his doubts had a purpose...finding the truth. He knew that finding the truth made one's faith stronger. Someone has said that doubt is one foot lifted, poised to step forward or backward. There is no motion until the foot comes down." We know where Thomas's foot came down from his statement concerning following Jesus, "Let us also go; that we may die with him". A lesson to be learned from Thomas is it is better to doubt out loud than to disbelieve in silence. God honors a searching heart.

We learn from Matthew that God takes our God-given skills and gives them eternal purpose when we follow him.

We need to remember that all things come from God. We need to remember, it is not what I can do, but rather, what God can do through a yielded heart.

We learn from Bartholomew, James the son of Alphaeues, Thaddaeus and Simon the Zealot that it matters not what men remember and record about our lives, what matters is what God has written in His Book. Those who are acclaimed by men in this life are but vehicles through which God can be glorified...individual rewards are a personal matter between individuals and God. We should all be seeking just a "Well done, thou good and faithful servant." Candidates for the Godly Man of the Year Award will not be seeking fame and fortune in this life, but will be faithful rejoicing to be in God's service, counted worthy by the Master.

ACTS 1:18,19; THE GOSPELS

JUDAS

Judas planned a wicked deed,
He will remain in infamy.
A bit of silver and a kiss,
The Pharisees' got their wish.

He had walked by Jesus' side,
But in his heart love did not reside
Fingers too long within the till,
Took control of Judas' will.

The other disciples never knew
What Judas planned to do.
They saw him leave the room
Forever to seal his doom.

When Judas allowed Satan in,
He betrayed his special friend.
As he looked into Jesus' eyes
Judas knew he had to die.

Judas took his own life,
While it was yet still night.
So close, and yet, so far.
To the Bright and Morning Star.

Not a puppet in God's plan,
Just a regular sort of man.
Accountable for each choice,
He heard not the Master's voice.

We shake our head and we say,
"How could he our Lord betray?"
But it's the same for all below,
Who do not Jesus know.

LESSONS FROM JUDAS

"The Devil is like a roaring lion, roaming about seeking whom he may devour." A fact Judas learned too late. Judas, like many of us, felt like Jesus needed a little help so he took matters into his own hands. He was not all that different from the other disciples in that he never quite understood all that Jesus said. He could not understand why they, the disciples had left everything if Jesus was not going to set up an earthly kingdom. He could not understand this "pie in the sky bye and bye stuff". Then there was the matter of his being in charge of the money bag. Whatever his motive we can see his situation was a fertile field for the roaring lion. Evil plans and motives leave us open to being used by Satan for even greater evil. Judas realized too late that the consequences of evil can be so devastating that even the smallest of lies, the most simple acts of wrong doing have great impact.

Judas made three major mistakes. First, he was greedy. Second, he betrayed Jesus for thirty pieces of silver. Third he, committed suicide instead of seeking forgiveness. The result, as in baseball, was "three strikes and you're out." We need to learn from Judas's experience that "it ain't over 'til it's over". Of course, we have the advantage of hindsight and history. In looking through the window of history we can see that all of the disciples in one way or another abandoned Jesus, which can be a form of betrayal. The difference comes in the action the disciples took in each of their respective situations. Judas saw that all hope was gone and hung himself from the nearest tree. We know that he felt remorse because he did not take the money and run. The other disciples gathered together probably as much out of fear as faith, but were able to gain at least some encouragement from one another. They basically were waiting to see what happens next. Waiting on God, even unintentionally, is always a good thing. Praying makes it even better for it is then that God will make His presence known. Once we focus back on Jesus, our sight becomes 20/20. We can see God's plan and His purposes working out even in the worst possible events.

A lesson to be learned from Judas is to forsake not the assembling of ourselves together, to confess our sins, to seek forgiveness, learn from our mistakes and surrender our lives to be all God wants us to be. This is the stuff of which Godly men are made.

LUKE 14:1-10

ZACCHAEUS (Pure/justified)

As Jesus went to and fro,
He entered into Jericho.
There He saw up in a tree,
A man too short to see.

Jesus looked above the crowd,
Then stated right out loud;
"Come down, for you see,
You will be a host to me!"

The people muttered as He went
They were troubled—discontent.
Why, did not Jesus know
Of this man from Jericho?

Zacchaeus was his name
Taxing gave him fame.
Rome had made him chief
At bringing Jews to grief.

Turncoat, traitor he was called
Hated by one and by all.
For by gouging below the belt,
He had amassed great wealth.

Love changed this little man
As only God's love can.
He then shared with the poor,
Paid back four times o'er.

This Son of Abraham was saved
In the one and only way.
By responding to the One
God called His Only Son.

LESSONS FROM ZACCHEUS

What I like about Zaccheus is that he recognized his need, sought the solution, took action, responded to the invitation, made restitution and reversed his course. He did all of this at great cost to his standing in the community, his finances, his family and his way of life. I love it that he did not ask his wife before he gave away the family fortune. One can only speculate as to her reaction. The fact that when Zaccheus came face to face with Jesus, nothing else mattered speaks volumes to those who desire to learn from his experience. Zaccheus's story is one of what happens when a turncoat turns around. His story is the prime example that when we meet the Master, the old life dies and a new life begins on that day.

Zaccheus was an opportunist. He was always looking out for number one. That is until he met the Master. Zaccheus was a Jew who looked around at the situation where he lived and moved himself into what he saw as the best vantage point in his changing culture. The Romans needed tax collectors. Zaccheus needed a career. The Romans had a going tax rate and gave the tax collectors carta blanc as to what they collected above and beyond that rate. Zaccheus had acquired great wealth at the expense of his neighbors and fellow countrymen. He was hated by both the Jews and the Romans. On the outside, he looked like everything was going his way… but the fact that he recognized he had a need tells us that beneath his mask there beat a broken heart. A heart that had a void that only God could fill. To his credit, Zaccheus took action. When he heard that Jesus was coming to town, he ran and climbed up a Sycamore tree just to get a glimpse of this man he knew only by reputation. Image his surprise when as Jesus passed by He stopped, looked up at Zaccheus and said, "Come down, for I am going to your house today."

Only Zaccheus and God know how often Zaccheus had prayed, not knowing to whom, for what God had in store for him on that day. Zaccheus wasted no time in getting out of the tree and into the arms of The Good Shepherd. The Good Shepherd wasted no time in taking Zaccheus into the fold. Someday we just may get to hear the rest of this story, but in the meantime, we can learn so much of God's Amazing Grace that is offered, not just to Zaccheus, but also to all who recognize their need, seek the solution, take action, respond to His invitation, make restoration and reverse their course. Marantha!

ACTS 7:58-28:31, THE EPISTLES

PAUL

T'was on the Damascus Road
Paul carried a heavy load.
He thought it was his job
To stop that "Christian" mob.

When to his great surprise,
God blinded both his eyes.
And the voice that he heard
Resounded throughout the earth.

For when God stops to ask why,
Your life will flash before your eye.
No longer could his lips be sealed,
God's truth had been revealed.

So in a stranger's house,
Paul shed all of his doubt.
To the Gentiles he would go,
Striving always God's grace to show.

Paul's life was carefully spent
On preaching, travel and making tents;
Writing letters which 'til this day
Help us to see and know God's way.

Paul was faithful when times were hard.
He shared God's love in prison garb.
The only time he lost his head,
Turned into a victory instead.

For it was upon that day,
He went home with Jesus to stay.
Paul had fought well the fight,
For him to live had been Christ!

LESSONS FROM PAUL

The old adage, "the road to hell is paved with good intentions", could be a good introduction into the lessons from Paul. Paul, in his own words, was the fairest of the Pharisees. He was very religious, note the word religious. It is not the same as being spiritual. He had the very best religious training, he had the very best of intentions, he thought he was right and that he knew the truth, he was very intense and zealous in his self appointed task to rid the world of this hated Christian faith. But, HE WAS WRONG!

You know the story; he was on his way to being successful in his task until he came face to face with Almighty God on the Road to Damascus. While up to this point, Paul had been spiritually blind, now his sight was taken from him. He had to be led to the house of a follower of Christ for help and instruction. How the mighty have fallen, or have they? What must have appeared as a disaster was in reality, the beginning of a great movement for Christ and Christianity. God was in the process of transforming a persecutor of Christians into a preacher for Christ! You see, God is in the transforming business. What He did for Paul, He can do for all who will receive Him. Paul left that little room to go throughout the Roman empire on three missionary journeys, planting churches, writing epistles, facing each and every issue or obstacle head on dealing with it. Paul learned to allow his strong personality to be bridled by Christ, taking him where God was leading.

God did not waste any part of Paul—his background, his training, his citizenship, his mind or even his weaknesses. It is the same for all who seek to be Godly. Candidates for the Godly Man of the Year Award need to learn from Paul to give all we are and hope to be over to God then allow Him to mold us into the vessel needed for our time.

We can learn also to never become so sure of ourselves and our motives that we cannot see the forest for the trees. Godly confidence for the tasks ahead come from being sure of the God we serve and being willing to learn from our mistakes. Paul also teaches us that there is no profit from over zealous remorse. We don't see where Paul fell into a pit of despair and guilt over his past actions. He accepted God's forgiveness and direction and moved forward in his faith and in his service. Once we have been forgiven our sin is forgotten by God and should be remembered by us only as a tool to move us forward not to render us ineffective. Godly men move forward to the calling for Christ.

ACTS 4:36,37; 9:27-15:39

BARNABAS (Son of Exhortation)

Barnabas was a friend to all,
But especially the Apostle Paul.
He had the special ability,
To see what a man could be.

He preached and won the lost,
No matter what price it cost.
He gave up the race for first,
Aiding others quenched his thirst.

When he saw one looking down,
He pointed up to Jesus' crown.
Barnabas put the fallen on their feet,
Taught them how to be complete.

The nickname of "Barnabas", Joseph earned,
For many a life was changed and turned,
After an encouraging touch or word,
From Barnabas was felt or heard.

Helping others took some risk,
Barnabas was not afraid of this.
One wonders what might have been,
Had he feared being Paul's friend.

Two journeys instead of one
More quickly got things done.
While others cut their loss,
Barnabas shared the cross.

LESSONS FROM BARNABAS

"No greater man of tongue can tell, than he who plays second fiddle well." This was to be Joseph's place in God's plan. In fact, he played his part so well that he was nick-named, Barnabas, which means Son of Encouragement by the people of the Jerusalem Church. That is the name we know him by today. Barnabas encouraged both the great and the small. He knew how and when to come alongside and walk with others. In fact, he was so good at this encouraging business that even non-believers flocked to his side.

It was Barnabas' encouragement that got the church to accept the Apostle Paul. It was Barnabas who encouraged Mark after he was discouraged in his mission endeavors. Barnabas patient encouragement was confirmed by the effective ministry of both Paul and Mark as well as the success in their missionary efforts. Barnabas was one of the first to sell his possessions to help the Christians in Jerusalem; he was Paul's first missionary partner. He is called an Apostle in scripture, no doubt because of his quiet influence on people during the early days of Christianity.

Look around you, there will always be someone in your sight who needs encouragement. Encouragement is one of the most effective tools we have to help others in their Christian faith and walk. Human nature tends to criticize rather than encourage. This tears down rather than building up. We are told that we are given Spiritual Gifts to build up the church. One of those gifts is the gift of encouragement. We often hear folks say, well I would love to help, but that is not my gift. All the gifts are also commands of God. We are to do all things in obedience and God will "gift" our efforts and obedience. We need to remember that the "gift" is the Holy Spirit working through us, not something we do in our own power. To God be the Glory. Barnabas may not have known a lot about Spiritual Gifts, he probably had never attended a conference on the subject. He just looked around, saw those who were discouraged and came alongside for as long as was needed.

Godliness can be seen in all acts of encouragement. Reach out an encourage someone today. God is watching.

MARK AND ACTS 13:13

MARK (The Lord is Gracious)

John Mark, a way back then,
Took up ink and a pen,
To record all that he heard,
Concerning Jesus our Lord.

He traveled with Barnabas and Paul,
Remembered all that he saw.
Peter was also his friend,
Right up until the end.

He stumbled once and failed,
But in the end, he prevailed.
John Mark did not shirk
When recording God's word.

Mark told of Jesus' power
And of death's final hour.
He wrote of sacrificial love,
Offered up from God above.

If you read Mark's words through,
Jesus becomes real to you.
You see Him as Man and Deity,
The One who died for you and me.

But the best thing he wrote,
Was how death's hold was broke.
When Jesus arose and was alive
Ascending from the mountain side.

Not unlike the disciples of old,
We should do as we are told,
Go and tell all men,
There is hope for them.

LESSONS FROM MARK

A lesson we can learn from Mark could be his sense of urgency. His favorite word was immediately! Now this was not always true of Mark. He had to reach the level of maturity to which he had arrived at the writing of the book bearing his name. It seems that Mark matured under the tutelage of Paul, Barnabas, Silas and Peter as they met in the home of his mother in Jerusalem.

~~~~~~~~~~~~~~~~~

Can't you just see the young man, possibly the same one who lost his clothes as he fled in fear at the time of Jesus' arrest, getting all fired up just being around all of the giants of the faith. One can only imagine the sights he saw, the conversations he heard or the answered prayers he witnessed. He was fired up and ready to go. Perhaps that accounts for some of his youthful mistakes. But we need to remember that personal maturity usually comes with time and a few mistakes. Mistakes can be great teachers if we take the time to learn from them. Mark's life is a prime example of how encouragement can change a person's life.

~~~~~~~~~~~~~~~~~

As Mark grew he wrote the second gospel, probably from Peter's first hand accounts. He persevered to become an assistant and traveling companion to three of the greatest early missionaries. The experiences during these mission trips could be where he got his sense of urgency in proclaiming the Gospel. As he matured he just may have learned that "time is a 'wastin." This is a lesson we can learn from Mark. We need to feel a sense of urgency in sharing the gospel of Jesus Christ. Mark seems to have seen that urgency lived out in the life of Jesus who knew His time was short upon this earth.

ACTS 16-28, LUKE, COLOSSIANS 4:14,
II TIMOTHY 4:11, PHILEMON 24

LUKE

Dr. Luke, a Gentile man,
Did the life of Jesus scan,
Then he recorded every word,
Exactly as he had heard.

The book of Luke bears his name,
Acts of the Apostles he made plain.
He made the people real,
Their joy and pain you can feel.

He told of miracles and of prayer,
Even of angels who were there.
Through his words we can see,
Jesus, the Man from Galilee.

Women have a special place,
As Gospel history he traced.
Paul was a close friend,
Luke was near 'til the end.

Luke affirmed Jesus' Deity,
Then showed forth His Humanity.
The only perfect man to be,
Came to save you and me.

On others Luke gave a detailed view,
But facts on him are very few.
What this says so plain to me
'Twas Jesus, Luke wanted us to see.

Self was put in a lesser place,
That he might reveal God's grace.
What better epitaph could be,
Than Jesus revealed by me.

LESSONS OF LUKE

Luke, or Dr. Luke, as I like to refer to him was a Gentile, probably Greek, physician from Antioch. He authored the gospel bearing his name and the book of Acts. He was a close friend and traveling companion of the Apostle Paul who referred to him as "beloved". Many believe that Dr. Luke was also Paul's physician citing the belief that Luke was with Paul during both of his imprisonments in Rome. Paul's reference that "only Luke is with me now" in II Timothy 4:11 also fosters this idea. Luke later adopted Philippi as his home after spending time there overseeing a church for Paul

Dr. Luke's writings reflect his profession. He had great compassion and attention to detail. He reveals the personal detail missing in the other Gospels. He seems to include more of the women and their trials than his counterparts. Many have said that the Gospel of Luke presents Mary's view while Matthew presents Joseph's interests. Luke stressed universal redemption available to all through Christ. His writings include Samaritans, pagan Gentiles, publicans, sinners and outcast. He teaches us that the rich and the poor are welcome in the kingdom along with the Jews and so called respectable people.

A reader of Luke's writings can almost feel this Godly man. His words reflect his being. We can learn from Dr. Luke to include everyone when we are sharing Christ. Christ died for all and is no respecter of persons. A Godly man will not withhold sharing God's grace any more than Christ would. A lesson we all need to learn is that in the eyes of Almighty God, we look the same when we come to Him, asking forgiveness. The only thing that makes us worthy is the blood of Jesus Christ

Another lesson for us is the attention to detail. Too often, we abbreviate the message assuming we are cutting to the chase, but the truth is every detail is important and needed in our walk with the Lord.

A final lesson from Luke is compassion. In his compassion he became the most Godly. We read where "Jesus had compassion". Compassion is more than acknowledging others situation. To have compassion like Jesus and Luke one must feel distress for the suffering of another with the desire to make things better...it is to feel the pain of others. Surely the Candidate for the Godly Man of the Year Award would have compassion for all.

GENESIS – REVELATION

SATAN

Lucifer was at one time,
An angel of the sublime.
He lived in heaven where,
God was always very near.

Lucifer let pride get in the way,
Tried a power play one day,
So God cast him down
To the earth's, cold cruel ground.

There he has spent his time,
Working hard upon his crime.
For Satan desires to be
Above The Sovereign Deity.

No longer bearing light,
He became a demon of the night.
Satan or Devil now he is called,
As he tries to destroy us all.

He works in subtle ways,
To try and lead us astray.
He gives us evil thoughts,
Unholy desires and wants.

Satan uses pride, anger and revenge,
Guilt and even mal-content.
He can make us very ill,
Ugly and weak-willed.

But God above is Supreme.
Satan's demise will be seen.
Into the abyss he will go
With death to hell below.

But until that final day,
Do not fail or betray
The Great and Only God above,

LESSONS FROM SATAN

Satan is the Father of all lies. He is also the master of disguise. He never knocks on our door and says, "Hi, I'm the devil, may I come in?" Oh he knocks on our doors, but always in disguise. He came to Adam and Eve as a snake and thus began his parade of costumes. Not only does he change his appearance, he also has a silver tongue. He likes to tickle our ears...tell us what we want to hear...make it easy to stray off the path of righteousness. If only he would come all dressed up in the red suit with a pitch fork in his hand. Man might have a better chance to resist his subtle suggestions and innuendos. But directness, truth and honor are foreign ideas to this demon.

Satan is a fallen angel. He once had a position of prominence in heaven. Pride overcame his perfect state and he desired to become a god. The God of Heaven cast him and others like him down to earth where he became the Chief of the Fallen Angels. He is also called the Adversary or enemy of God. Prophecy foretells his demise at the return of Jesus, but not before great desolation, sorrow and pain. He is called the evil one and devil in scripture. We learn in the book of Job that he communicates with God and that God allows him to do certain things as evidenced in the life of Job. His presence is the stirring pot for all of man's rebellion against God.

Satan's greatest weapon is man's pride and desire for control. It is a characteristic he shares. As has been proven time and time again, pride goes before a fall. It causes the demise of both man and demons.

The lesson we can learn from Satan is beware, your sins will find you out. Literally! Out of step with God, out of the family and out of eternal life with Jesus. We can learn to long for the Truth and to beware of ear tickling. The most important lesson we can learn is to have a personal relationship with our Lord and Savior and be so intimately involved in His will that we don't even hear ole Satan a 'nocking on our door. We can be so aware of the Truth that the Lie will be evident and avoided. We can learn to stay so focused on the One that thought we were to die for that we can see no other.

GENESIS-REVELATION

JESUS

Jesus is the Bright and Morning Star,
who one day will go to war
With the redeemed by His side.
He will "tan" ole Satan's hide.
Jesus is God's only Son, the One you can count upon.
For He has proved His love, by coming down from above.

He left His glory far behind, to help us all He resigned.
He walked on earth as a man, it was a part of God's plan.
Jesus redeems us all if we upon His name will call.
T'was on ole Calvary's tree, He paid for you and for me.

Jesus had a virgin birth, to begin His work upon earth.
A manager was His bed, no place to lay His head.
He went to church as a youth, taught the elders of the Truth.
Then in His thirtieth year, He knew His time was near.

So He went to the River Jordan,
to be baptized by His cousin.
'Twas then God sent down a dove as a sign of His love.
Then Jesus chose twelve men to be of a help to Him;
He taught them the Truth, so it could be passed to you.

Jesus healed the sick and the blind,
always busy — so little time
He fed the hungry, walked upon the water,
then taught them of His Father.
Jesus of His death foretold,
but his friend's response was cold.
For they did not understand, '
Twas love that redeemed man.

Jesus broke the bread as He gently said;
"Eat henceforth and think of me; I will die to set you free."
Then He took the cup, and said; "Drink it up!
This will help you see the blood belonged to me."

Jesus at the close of day went into a garden to pray.
He asked others to pray and watch,
but asleep they were caught.
Jesus said to sleep awhile, as His foes planned His trial.
Then He received Judas' kiss; things took on an ugly twist.

Not a word did He speak, all around others shrieked.
Silent as a little Lamb, He accomplished God's plan.
He was hung upon a tree, in the midst of two thieves,
Seven things Jesus said, then it was dark, He was dead.

continued

God had turned away His face;
He could not look upon this place.
For the sins of all men were piled high upon Him.
Gently, Joseph took Jesus down,
buried Him within the ground.
His followers were not there. All around was despair.

The enemy alone believed, Jesus words they received.
Something about the third day,
they made sure He would stay.
A soldier and a stone, Jesus dead and all alone,
Then at the break of day, God rolled the stone away.

Jesus is alive forevermore, glorious things He has in store.
The women to the tomb came, angels had to explain.
Jesus appeared to many then, helping them to understand
The victory had been won, now He was going home.

But if He went, He'd come again,
when the time was right for man.
If we but on Him believe He'll take us home
with Him when day is done.
But until that great day, His Spirit will guide the way.
Stay busy at your task, that is all that Jesus asks.

LESSONS FROM JESUS

Because we are born into sin, that is separated from God because of the sin of Adam and Eve, God looked down and because He loved us found a way to bring us back home; back into a right relationship with Him. "For God so loved the world that He gave His only begotten Son, that whosoever believeth in Him might be saved." So Jesus, out of love and of His own choice came to earth leaving all of His divinity behind and became one of us that He might die in our place to justify us before the Father. God cannot abide with sin so Jesus took all of our sins, past, present and future upon Himself and won the victory over death through His rejection, suffering, death and resurrection. But we have a part in that process. That part is recognition of our hopeless state, our need, then acceptance of God's gift of Grace, His Son, Jesus. We then need to confess our sins (separation from God) and invite Jesus into our hearts to become the Lord and Master of our Life. The next step is to nurture that personal relationship through learning about God, listening to God, talking with God and sharing God with others.

Jesus taught, "I am the Way, the Truth and the Life. No one comes to the Father, but by me." It's a lesson! Learn it!

Jesus taught, "Come unto me all ye who are weary, and I will give you rest." It's a lesson! Learn it!

Jesus taught, "Repent for the Kingdom of Heaven is at hand." It's a Lesson! Learn it!

Jesus taught, "Love one another; for by this shall all men know that you are my disciples." It's a lesson! Learn it!

Jesus taught, "Follow me! It's a lesson! Learn it!

Jesus taught, "Go ye, therefore and make disciples of all nations, baptizing them in the name of the Father and the Son and the Holy Spirit." It's a lesson! Learn it!

Jesus taught, "Keep watching and praying, that you may not come into temptation; the spirit is willing, but the flesh is weak." It's a lesson! Learn it!

Jesus taught, "Let not your heart be troubled, believe in God; believe also in me." It's a lesson! Learn it!

Jesus taught, "If I go, I will come again." It's a lesson! Learn it!

Jesus taught, "Today, you shall be with me in Paradise." It's a lesson! Learn it!

Jesus taught, "Watch, for the night is coming". It's a lesson! Learn it!

Jesus prayed, "Into thy hands I commend my spirit…" It's a prayer! Pray it!

POSTLOGUE

—ɯ—

One last thing that for me sums up God's message for all today comes from a song popular during World War II. It is…

"DON'T SIT UNDER THE APPLE TREE

WITH ANYONE ELSE BUT ME

'TILL I COME MARCHING HOME?"

See you under the tree! God Bless you in your quest to Godliness!

CPSIA information can be obtained at www.ICGtesting.com
Printed in the USA
LVOW13s1302020414

380000LV00003B/3/P